That's Life

THAT'S LIFE

LIFE

MARTY WHELAN

GILL & MACMILLAN

Gill & Macmillan
Hume Avenue
Park West
Dublin 12
www.gillmacmillanbooks.ie

978 07171 6826 2

Edited by Alison Walsh
Printed and bound by the CPI Group (UK) Ltd, Croydon, CRO 4YY

Photo of the Monkees on p.38 © Getty Images.

This book is typeset in Sabon LT.

The paper used in this book comes from the wood pulp of managed forests. For
every tree felled, at least one tree is planted, thereby renewing natural resources.

5 4 3 2 1

To Lily and Sean (Mam and Dad)
and to Maria, Jessica and Thomas,
all the loves of my life.
Love you all to the moon and back.

ABOUT THE AUTHOR

Marty Whelan was born in Dublin in 1956. Frequently seen and heard on RTÉ radio and television, he has presented a variety of shows including *Open House*, *Winning Streak* and, for 15 years in a row, the Eurovision Song Contest. His popular weekday Lyric FM show, *Marty in the Morning*, features an upbeat mix of craic, banter, risqué jokes and great music to put a spring in your step. He lives in Malahide, Co. Dublin with his wife, Maria, and two children, Jessica and Thomas.

ACKNOWLEDGEMENTS

Along the way there are people who make a difference in your life. They are often people who are with you on a project, it ends, and then we all move on. Sadly, keeping in touch can be difficult because schedules can be different and you lose touch with people you don't mean to. Well, I have worked with many marvellous people, inside and outside RTÉ, and acknowledge them with real warmth. But in a career spanning the bones of forty years, there's bound to be the odd lapse in memory ... so rather than set out a list of names and forget you (that wouldn't be nice!), you know who you are. Thank you from the bottom of my heart.

To my new friends at Gill & Macmillan – to Nicki Howard, for believing in me and pushing the project through with such style. To Alison Walsh, my editor, who to her horror realised with quiet acceptance that I hate deadlines; she was super and made the process so much easier for me. To Jen Patton, in charge of all my photos – why can't I include 370? Your patience I admire and for ensuring Buddy made it, warm thoughts. To Catherine Gough, for keeping it all on track, and Teresa Daly, for managing all the promo so efficiently, many thanks. To Dave Verschoyle, for showing me all I now know about writing technology, but not all he knows. He made it possible for me to speak my thoughts into a microphone and have them magically appear on the page before me. He's a wizard!

To colleagues, past and present, at PMPA, back in the day, at RTÉ since 1979, Century Radio, Lyric FM and the National Lottery. I hope we had some laughs along the way.

And finally, to you, for listening to me on the radio since 1977 and watching me on television since 1983. I thank you with all of my heart. It's been a glorious journey with more ups than downs and I couldn't have done it without you.

INTRODUCTION

It never occurred to me that one day I would be asked to pen my memoirs; the idea that my story is in any way significantly different than that of others of my background just never crossed my mind. But as the years passed, and I found myself in unusual situations, I would think to myself, 'how lucky am I?' In fact, how different my life might have been. Then, in the space of a couple of years I was asked three times to think about the possibility of writing a book. Flattered though I was, I delayed the decision for a few reasons. First, I wasn't really ready to go down that road. Then, was there enough to tell?

Well, Nicki Howard from Gill & Macmillan thought so and convinced me to undertake the project. It's been an interesting journey down memory lane for me, recalling happy, sad, trying and successful events in my life. This is all me, from the heart. I sat at my desk putting down my memories onto each page. I hope you enjoy it as much as I enjoyed writing it.

That's it ... That's life. My life.

THE EARLY YEARS

'Dancing in the Dark'

Bruce Springsteen

Leaving my parents' house on the morning of 13 August 1985 felt like a monumental affair. I'd called that house home for all of my 29 years, so not being able to do so ever again was an odd sensation somehow. In my trendy black suit, grey waistcoat, bow tie and shiny shoes, I was the picture of manly elegance. (Actually, I still have the trousers, not out of any foolish belief that they might actually fit me, so heaven knows why; in fact, they'll never have contact with my legs again!) This was my wedding day and I was leaving my mum and dad for the last time. I was finally growing up, marrying my childhood sweetheart, Maria, the girl I'd met at a dance in Clontarf in the heady days of 1974.

Monumental indeed, but it had been that kind of year, 1985. Mikhail Gorbachev had become General Secretary of the Communist Party in March, a hole in the ozone layer was discovered in May, and July brought Live Aid and the chance for Phil Collins to play two concerts on either side of the Atlantic on the same day, thanks to Concorde. All of this, of course, paling into insignificance in August when I stepped down the aisle with the girl of my dreams. What was it Gilbert O'Sullivan wrote in his song 'Matrimony'? 'Marriage, the joining together of two people, for better or for worse. Till death them do part. Olé!' But I'll come back to that later.

In fact, marrying Maria was the second momentous event of 1985 for me. The first happened on 1 June that year when The Boss, Bruce Springsteen, came to Slane. He had never played to such a capacity crowd; some would later say it was over 100,000 fans, and Maria and I were lucky enough to be among them. He became a global superstar on that evening in June by the banks of the Boyne. As the opening strains of 'Born in the USA' played and the band marched forward like conquering heroes, we all knew we were witnessing something special in music history. Later on, a friend and I, ably helped along by copious amounts of refreshments from the backstage bar, decided to see if we could purloin (take without paying for, remove discreetly, okay, steal!) a souvenir of the day. We were duly spotted by the girders behind the stage holding a small table flower arrangement, which we'd 'lifted' from backstage. Words were superfluous and, quite frankly, I can't recall what we said by way of explanation. I'm absolutely sure, though, even we wouldn't have understood our own words at that time and we were sent off with a flea in our respective ears. Funny thing is, we then spotted a chair that Bruce might have sat on earlier on: explain the carrying of that through the bushes of Slane to a burly bouncer, will you? Ah, the things we did, or nearly did in this case. I would love to divulge the name of the individual who accompanied me on this Springsteen episode but alas and alack, as Spike Milligan once said, I am taken agad. It wouldn't be right to impugn the unsullied-until-now reputation of a senior member of RTÉ management. However, should the opportunity arise and I need to use this in some way to further my career prospects, I will of course hold back, because that is not the sort of fellow I am.

Ah, yes, but where was I now? Getting married ... I suppose the most unusual thing about getting married, for me at least, was the fact that I had never been married before. You might say to yourself, Is that a problem? After all, if you've never been married before and all seems well with those around you who are, then why should you feel any sense of concern? And the good news is, I didn't; it was just that it was all going to be quite new to me. Maria and I had never lived away from home, me as an only child, Maria with her folks and five siblings. We had never moved out into a flat or that sort of mad studenty thing. We'd been with students over the years and had the fun and we had some sense of what it's like not to live at home. All that, 'Who bought the milk?' All that, 'What do you mean, we've no bread?' All that, 'Don't tell me you want to play Leonard Cohen again?' No, we had had the sedate joy that is living with the mammy and the daddy and the fact that no matter what happened, there would always be bread, milk and, quite frankly, if you wanted to play Mickey Cohen, no one would have batted an eyelid. And yet it felt right and it was right.

Meantime, back to the getting married bit, it really is quite the day, isn't it? Quite apart from the newness of leaving home, for me it was all about organisation; about making sure that everything from your end is as it supposed to be, but from the bride's point of view, it was a completely different situation. For her it was all about making sure everything was absolutely perfect, and I mean perfect! I suppose for me, the event itself brought its own issues. For a start, as an only child, as I am, you don't automatically have a best man; you've got to find one. Now, I was lucky I had friends in abundance and any number of fine capable young lads would do the job just perfectly. I had the good fortune to ask one of my longest-standing friends. God bless you, Robbie Irwin.

Actually it's funny, but Robbie and I met in Seal Records, on Marlborough Street, just around the corner from Dolphin Discs, back in the mid-seventies. I think the place where Stan used to supply all the aspiring DJs with the latest waxings is now a phone shop and Seal Records has turned into some sort of restaurant. Robbie and I became firm friends and worked together for over 15 years. He is a well-known sports broadcaster in RTÉ, you know, and one of the finest fellows it's ever been my pleasure to know. So we had Robbie as best man, Willie Kavanagh as groomsman and we were all set with the shiny shoes and the best bib and tucker. Maria had her sister Karen as her bridesmaid and her sister-in-law Marguerite as maid of honour. Quite the little troupe.

The diminutive actor Mickey Rooney, married eight times and therefore somewhat of an expert, once said, 'Always get married early in the morning. That way, if it doesn't work out, you haven't wasted a whole day.' Then there was the other great line, not from Mickey Rooney: 'My wife and I were happy for 20 years, then we met.' But none of this was the case, nor would prove to be the case. We had a most marvellous day: the sun shone, the music played, love was in the air and my wife was radiant. Happy, happy day.

We had our reception in a wonderful location, the Beaufield Mews, a restaurant in Stillorgan, Co. Dublin, which was originally a coach house and stables, but which now housed antiques upstairs, with a fine restaurant downstairs and its own lush garden with flowers in abundance. We enjoyed fine food and wine and were surrounded by family and friends. Funny, as I tell you this, I can still see my parents, Lily and Sean, and Maria's parents, Kathleen and Tom, now all gone, getting on so well and thoroughly enjoying the day. It was very unusual in those days to be able to have the run of the place, which made it particularly special. Another thing that was special about the day was the fact that Maria, the bride, decided to speak and welcome everyone, and, much to my alarm, told the assembled multitude that our home was to be an open house for family and friends from now on ... she wasn't wrong there.

Because Mrs Whelan (newly crowned) and I had travelled a little bit by then, thanks to her job as an air hostess in Aer Lingus, we decided the menu should perhaps offer something a little out of the ordinary. So the culinary genius at the venue agreed to oblige and we served up veal as a main course. It was lovely, it really was, and everybody seemed to enjoy it tremendously. Of course this gave best man Robbie the opportunity to thank us for the lovely bit of fish! So now you can see the sort of tone that was being set.*

We had our old friend Vincent Hanley, God bless him, and our best girlfriend Pauline doing the entire Aer Lingus pre-take-off safety drill as an impromptu entertainment. Vincent really would have been such a good steward. I also feel it necessary to make note of other guests at our wedding: my old pal, Ireland's resident singing Argentinian, Chris de Burgh and his lady in red, Diane, along with her babe in arms, Rosanna. Now hang on a second here, I realise that is all very fine for the hoi polloi to be able to say things about how marvellous their social circle is, but how many among us can say that he had Miss World at his

---

* Here's a great gag about fish. There's a man standing on the corner, and he's yelling, 'Roll up, roll up; for five euro I will show you a man-eating fish.' You pay your fiver, go round the corner and there's a man sitting at an outdoor restaurant with a plate of cod in front of him. Meantime our friend has done a runner with your fiver!

wedding? Say what you will, it happened to us. The mad thing is, years later, when I was compère of the Miss Ireland pageant (one way or another I've been everywhere) it was I who announced on the stage that Rosanna Davison was the new Miss Ireland. So I am feeling a link here.

It really was such a special day and I look back on it with great fondness. We loved having everybody we had at the wedding and yet there are so many people I suppose we would like to have asked ... but it's easy to look back and you have to let things like that go. The important thing is that so many friendships from that day have endured.

Thankfully, other things haven't endured, such as the fashions. When I think about what the sprightly lad was offered in that department: the high-waisted trousers for a start (now more of a necessity than then), the nicely fitted shirt, shoes of the slip-on variety with tassels on them, and I was all set. And when I look back to that period, I wasn't the only one sporting the old moustache, or, as they say in running circles, must dash! Back then, there were quite a few of us with them, but now I'm practically the only one. (I wouldn't be the same without it and quite frankly, it's grown on me – gotcha!)

When it came to the girls, there seemed to be a lot of colour about – well, it was August. We must remember the era we're talking about here, the mid-eighties, and the world of *Dynasty* and *Dallas*, which meant that flowery frocks abounded and hair, for those who had enough of

it, was of the bouffant variety, not forgetting the big shoulders. Shoulders that seemed to me to make it possible for
girls to play in the position of quarterback on any college
team in America. At any social gathering, you would see
long flared skirts, jumpsuits, bolero jackets, Lycra everywhere … you'd hardly think a fellow would notice the
stuff, but I think it's because both my parents were in the
rag trade. My father, Sean, had spent most of his working
life in Clery's department store on O'Connell Street, while
my mam, Lily, until she had me, had worked in Cassidy's
clothes shop on South Great George's Street. Sure wasn't I
only steeped in *haute couture*. Indeed, one radio colleague
said to me, 'You're the only man I know who dresses for
radio.' Can't help it, has to be done. When you dress up,
you feel better about yourself and I think it gives you a
sense that you give whatever you're doing a better shot.
When you get up in the morning, if your shirt is crisp, your
trousers pressed, you have a bit of a shine on the old shoes,
you're off, set up for the day. To this day I can rarely pass
Louis Copeland on Pembroke Street without going in and
purchasing something from Adrian and his smiling crew.*

✱ Which brings me to a joke. Now, hold on to something solid for
this one, from Glen Ribbeen, one of my morning crew. An
Englishman, an Irishman, a Welshman, a Gurkha, a Latvian, a Turk,
an Aussie, a German, a Yank, an Egyptian, a Japanese, a Mexican, a
Spaniard, a Russian, a Pole, a Lithuanian, a Jordanian, a Kiwi, a Swede,
a Finn, a Canadian, an Israeli, a Romanian, a Bulgarian, a Serb, a Swiss,
a Greek, a Singaporean, an Italian, a Norwegian, an Argentinian, a
Libyan, a Muslim, a Hindu, a Buddhist and an African went to a nightclub. The bouncer said, 'Sorry, I can't let you in without a Thai.' God
bless my merry band of early risers; without them I'd be lost.

Meantime, back to the honeymoon. Did anybody mention it before now? You would think that having married an air hostess, there would be an element of the marriage, or at least of the beginning of the marriage, that would go according to some plan. Let me stop you there; that's not how it went. We took a plane – it's the only way to fly – to London after an overnight in a secret location – Moyglare Manor in Maynooth – for our first night of wedded bliss, and at Heathrow we basically looked to see what was available. As Maria worked for Aer Lingus, we were travelling on standby, hoping to go to the Caribbean paradise of St Lucia; instead, because the flight was full, it turned out to be the Italian paradise of Milan, which was fortunate, really, because had it turned out to be Anchorage, Alaska, our summer holidays for the next number of decades would have turned out very differently.

We flew to Milan with not a care in the world, nor a bed booked. 'And tell me, Mart, what month did you go to Milan?' I hear you say. Ah, well, let me see, that would be August.

'You mean, the month that Milan closes down?'

The very one.

You know, it's at times like this that you realise your good fortune in marrying an air hostess. It turned out to be a great plan, even though it wasn't a plan at all, by virtue of the fact that we hired a car and headed off to Lago

Maggiore and quite simply had the best time. In fact, we fell in love with Italy. And that love, like our own, has stayed with us throughout our lives. Every time we return to Italy, we both feel a sense of belonging, a sense of homecoming, a sense of … maybe it's the wine!

Looking back on that inauspicious beginning to our Italian adventure, I'm now trying to recall the places we've been in Italy: Rome, Ischia, Capri, Sperlonga, Naples, Turin, Sorrento, Milan, Positano, Venice, Verona *et al*. A number of these have required return trips over the years, in case we might have missed a bit. That's the wonderful thing about visiting Italy: it never ceases to enthral and amaze and delight and each trip is filled with the excitement of some new discovery: the very idea of hiring a car and driving along the Amalfi coast, with its wonderful views, listening to Giuseppe Di Stefano or Pavarotti on the CD player as the wind blows through your hair (that, my friend, probably deserves an entire chapter to itself: the hair, not the driving). And just for good measure we have also included Sicily in our plans. Flying to Catania one year we stayed in Taormina, where we chanced upon the film festival. We knew nobody, but it didn't matter: everybody looked like a star, even the fellas driving the cars. Especially them. That's the thing about the Italians: when there's something on, they put on their best bib and tucker and sally forth like millionaires and you can see where that gets them! (I like to think that it's their languid demeanour. As one of my *Marty in the Morning* listeners remarked recently: 'I say, Marty, old boy, I had a languid demeanour once. You can get a cream to sort it out though!')

And while we are on the topic of Italians, there is a great capacity for the limerick on the radio show: it seems to get the juices flowing early on. One such came when Ennio Morricone, or as my listener, Mr F Donnelly from Donabate, likes to refer to him, Eamon Macaroni, played in Dublin:

> There was a young man from Rome,
> On a Vespa with gleaming new chrome,
> He shot round the forum,
> With dashing decorum,
> And landed on St Peter's Dome!

...

Even though I'd known Maria for 11 years at this stage, starting a new chapter in our lives was very exciting. Any new direction in life, no matter what it is, personal or professional, is bound to bring great hope and expectation and a sense that this is the right thing to do, this is a new way to be, and so off we went, Maria and me, to take on board the most profound change imaginable – being married. We were suddenly being grown up, in charge of our own destinies, making decisions about ourselves, from the very basics, such as whether we had enough milk, because there was no one else to get it, to the bigger things. Responsibility arrived, I am reliably informed, yet we were only in our late twenties: what an adventure. The fact that we came from very different home lives, me as an only child and Maria as one of six, could have caused issues for us, but it felt right and it was right.

There is always that memory that stays with me of the two of us in our new house, *our* home, before the furniture had arrived and before we'd actually really decorated, sitting on the floor in the front room with a Chinese takeaway on a cardboard box in front of us and a bottle of the finest wine of its time, le Piat D'Or, a vintage of dubious quality. (There used to be an ad on the telly for this feisty red, 'The French adore le Piat D'Or'. I doubt the French would let it inside the door.) Well, we thought we'd finally arrived. This would be our home for the next 25 years. As Burt Bacharach and Hal David once wrote (in fact, it was Hal David who wrote all the lyrics), 'A House is not a Home', but ours was. Maria would make it one, because it's just her way.

...

But back to Bruce, the other big event of my life in 1985. I'm trying to remember when I became a fan of his and I'm pretty sure it was from the get-go. There is an amazing song on the first album, *The Wild, the Innocent and the E-Street Shuffle*, called 'Fourth of July, Asbury Park (Sandy)'. It's quiet and contemplative and Bruce paints a wonderful picture, like a good poet should. Then there's the raw energy of 'Rosalita', a song that rocks still, over 40 years later. In a way, I was with Bruce before Miami Steve turned up, but don't tell him: if you've seen *The Sopranos* or *Lilyhammer* on the telly, you will know why I'd like to keep this between you and me. You see, there are a number of songwriters who can give you that warm glow and then rock with the best of them. Van Morrison, Phil Lynott, Elton John and a few other carefully chosen ones. Bruce epitomises it, he just does.

I recall years ago when I was on the ten-to-midnight slot on 2fm, I got to play all the rocky songs that Bruce would record and sometimes, in the comfort of my own studio, I would find myself dancing to him. Betimes, I would be aided in this onerous task by my producer Pat Dunne (there you are, another dancing partner exposed). On the subject of dancing, years after that Slane concert, I had the good fortune to be asked by the lovely Jim Aiken, the promoter, to act as DJ with Mark Cagney at a Fourth of July party for Bruce Springsteen in Carton House in Maynooth. We were like children, the pair of us, as The Boss, Miami Steve, Clarence Clemens, God be good to him, *et al* partied on. All Bruce wanted was for us to play some Roy Orbison. Now, you have to remember, gentle reader, that this was in the day of the single, the trusty old 7-inch, the tool of the DJ's trade. Basically we had two boxes of singles and, as far as we were concerned, we were totally covered for all eventualities; but we hadn't counted on Bruce. However, luckily we had one song by Roy Orbison, 'Only the Lonely', and we must have played it half a dozen times for him. The joy of the moment was captured on film by Mark's late wife Anne when I asked Bruce to dance and, shockingly, he accepted. I have to be honest and say I have danced with the odd man before, some odder than others, but that was in the interest of friendship and a laugh. This, however, was Bruce Springsteen. We clasped hands and went for it; he is quite the mover, as you may be aware. Anne clicked, we smiled, I held The Boss close to me and the last we saw of our hero was him running off singing

'Only the lonely, dumb dumb dumb dummy doo wah,' before jumping headlong into a hedge.*

No matter what show I've done on the radio over the years, Bruce Springsteen always seems to feature. Happy songs, sad songs, straight-out rock songs and gentle ballads, not forgetting the huge catalogue of songs that tell the story of America then and now. He's a working man's hero, loved by male and female alike. In fact, over the last number of years, he certainly seems to be working out. I notice this, of course, as our physique would be quite similar. No laughing in the cheap seats now! His music is wonderful but he always sets out to tell a story; many of them about the little man fighting back, about the guy who goes the wrong way but tries to do the right thing. This is the Bruce Springsteen I've loved for all these years. He is The Boss, after all. What is it about this New Jersey link I have? I'm also a maniac for Hoboken native Frank Sinatra. But what makes Bruce exceptional is the duration of his concerts and the energy of them. He never goes out half-cocked, it is always full on and always as strong as it can be; he never waivers. I think that's why when you go to see most other people of his ilk, you feel like asking, when they finish, hang on a second lads, isn't there any more? With Bruce, you leave exhausted after three plus hours.

---

* Speaking of hedges, I've always loved the gag about hedgehogs from the Edinburgh Fringe of years ago. 'Hedgehogs. Why can't they just share the hedge?' That's one of those gags that stays with you.

How does he do it night after night? Now, don't be making up your own jokes.*

It was Martin Luther King Jr, no stranger to quotes himself, who quoted Douglas Malloch; 'If you can't be a highway, just be a trail; if you can't be the sun, be a star; for it isn't by size that you win or you fail – be the best of whatever you are.' Stirring words, indeed, and they certainly apply to Bruce.

I recall that when the great concert promoter Jim Aiken died in February 2007, I couldn't get to the funeral because of work, so I met up with Gerry Ryan that day, also sadly gone to the great gig in the sky, and the car was organised and off we went to Jim's removal in Belfast. Along the way we talked of many things, having laboured in school together and subsequently in RTÉ. But the journey was about paying tribute to the man, a man of high standing, a man of high standards, indeed one of the finest men it has been my pleasure to know. We paid our respects to his lovely wife Anne, his son Peter and family, then made our

 All of which reminds me of a limerick:
There was a young man called Bruce,
Who enjoyed letting it loose,
He jumped on the stage,
Quite fit for his age,
Slipped and now lives in a caboose.

That came from the dark recesses of my radio mind, no doubt sent by somebody I woke up inadvertently on the wireless recently.

way back to Dublin. It was right and proper that we made the journey and I'm so glad I have the memory of Gerry and me paying respect to and acknowledging this fine man.

At Jim's funeral there were many accolades and fine tributes – among the congregation was a certain country singer named Garth Brooks, that says it all – but a letter was read out from Bruce Springsteen and it wasn't about business or about money earned or about the fact that that day back in Slane in 1985, when Jim Aiken promoted him, turned him into a world superstar; it was simply to say that his family felt crushed. 'Such a big part of the joy we feel when we come to Ireland is seeing that big grin of yours when we come off stage.' That was what he remembered, a very human side of the business and the pleasure and indeed the warmth that existed between the two men. Now there's the measure of a man.

So 1985 was a highlight for me in seeing one of my great heroes live on stage, but more than that, in marking the beginning of a new life with the girl I'd known for 11 years. I'll tell you all about meeting Maria later in the book, but she was, and is, a soulmate, a friend and a guide. Without her, 1985 and the years that followed just wouldn't have been the same.

'Mama'

Dave Berry

What is it about the Irish mammy? Now, all mammies are different, we know that, but there is a fundamental kindness in the Irish mammy, a streak of auld decency that transcends everything else. Hence the well-worn phrase that, when the lights have gone out and a bulb needs changing, the Irish mammy will say: 'Don't mind me, son, I'll just sit here in the dark.' For much of my mam's life, that was how she operated: only in her dotage, when she became quite unwell, did she accede to being minded. She was one of the greatest women I ever met. Having her for as long as I did meant that she was a part of every aspect of my life until she died in October 2013 at the age of 95, a day after her birthday. Being an only child – me, not her – meant no decision was made in our lives without us being aware of its impact on her, and so much of the person I am today I owe to her; indeed, to both my parents.

Mam was born Elizabeth Doheny on 8 October 1918 in Kilbeggan, Co. Westmeath, into a changing Ireland. The family subsequently moved to Athlone, which is really where Mam remembered her childhood spent on Goldsmith Terrace. She was the youngest of five children, three girls and two boys, and lived in the shadow of the local convent, as she always said, 'under the watchful eye of the nuns'. She was incredibly close to her mother, who instilled a sense of self-belief in her that stood her in good stead all her life. This was a trait she passed on to me, which is handy when you get the odd disappointment in life. Let's face it, if you don't believe in yourself, who will?

Like many other Irish children at the time, there was a possibility that my mam could have been adopted by her maiden aunt in America, Auntie May. But there was no way she would have left her family, even though this could have opened up a whole new world for her. The idea of going to America with a relative was not unusual at the time, when Irish families were big and often not very well off, but even though Mam turned down the opportunity, she remained in close contact with her aunt all her life.

When Mam was 13, her elder sister Josie moved to Dublin. Mam went to visit her some time later and during the visit got talking to a friend of her sister's, who also worked in Cassidy's of South Great George's Street, and she was asked if she'd be interested in working there. A meeting was arranged with the manager, the interview happened and, lo and behold, she was offered the job starting the following Monday. This all seems very fast, I know, but it's how Mam related it to me.

When she went back to Athlone to tell her parents her good news, they were a bit shocked. Neither of them wanted her to move up to Dublin, of course. She was only 13. But her mum, knowing how keen she was on the new job, said to her dad, 'Let her go, John, she will be home within the week.' But she wasn't. This was the start of the rest of her life. In time, her parents moved to Dublin and the family ended up back together again, but Mam continued to work in Cassidy's. She eventually became a buyer of ladies' clothes and, as you'll have learned from my wedding day, I do love a well-cut suit. (Time, I think, to cue the old Tommy Cooper joke: My wife was looking through a fashion magazine and she saw a fur coat. She said: 'I want that.' So I cut it out and gave it to her. Indeed.)

Now, Mam apparently had many suitors – remember, this was a time when, if you gave somebody a kiss, you nearly had to get engaged! In the shop working alongside my mam was Kay Whelan (a mean piano player, as I recall). One day, my mother called to their house in Kilmainham and met Kay's brother, Sean Whelan, the man of her dreams – well, that's how my father described it years later. A Dubliner, he was born in Kilmainham on 8 April 1920. He was working at the time in Troy's, also of George's

Street, a gents' outfitters, moving then to Clery's department store in O'Connell Street, where he would remain for the next 36 years, in the shirt department for most of the time, elevated to the position of floor walker. For those of you not familiar with the term (or who don't remember Mr Peacock in *Are You Being Served?*), a floor walker answered customer queries, co-signed cheques and listened patiently to complaints. So the pair of them had the rag trade in common.

Now, the relationship had its ups and downs early on. Circumstances kept them apart and then they went their separate ways for a bit and Mam had gentlemen callers aplenty, but none came close to my dad. Apparently she did a novena around this time and during the ceremony, prayed for an opportunity to see my dad again. As she was walking down O'Connell Street one day, she spotted a tall man in a long coat and a hat. Her heart skipped a beat, according to herself, as she kept walking closer and closer. When he turned around, she saw it was my dad. He asked her out on the spot, she accepted, they courted for another year and then he proposed to her on the Hill of Howth and she accepted. They got married on 12 July 1955 and went on honeymoon to Port Stewart in Northern Ireland.

Have you noticed anything significant about the date? Yes, you guessed it, they decided to go on their honeymoon on the biggest day of the Orange parades in the North. Not only that, but my dad was sporting his Pioneer pin on the lapel of his jacket. One taxi driver said to him, 'You may want to take that off, just in case of bother.' When I think of the innocence of the pair of them, it's actually quite sweet.

They stayed in a hotel called The Strand; I'm guessing it was on the beach. My mam kept the brochure for the hotel all her life and, as a result, I can tell you that in 1955, the hotel was equipped with central heating and hot and cold running water was available in all 100 bedrooms, which also had electric light and all modern conveniences for the comfort of visitors. It even had service phones and landings! Another notice in the brochure should bring a smile to your face: 'lights out in corridors at 12 midnight'. Why? What did they think you'd be up to in the corridor after midnight?

...

My mam was 29 when she lost her mother in 1947 and the effect on her was very great. She had been incredibly close to her mother and when she passed away, Mam devoted herself to looking after her dad. Into this world came my dad and they set up house in the family home in Killester. They got a mortgage and settled down. And then, a year after their marriage, in 1956, the most amazing thing happened, the most fabulous, joyful, magnificent event that could occur, occurred ... I was born – I always say Under a Wanderin' Star, but no – in the National Maternity Hospital in Holles Street, on 7 June 1956. According to her, I was a perfect baby: I never cried and based on the praise she heaped on me to anyone within earshot, you would think I never even had a dirty nappy. I'm sure she was right.

Sadly, there were three miscarriages after me, so I was the only child, son and heir. Of course, this must have been very difficult for Mam, and even though it wasn't something she kept secret, neither herself nor Dad really dwelt on it. It was the way in those days, I suppose, to just get on with life. Mam became a full-time housewife and minder of my dad, and my dad continued working in Clery's. We were a very happy gang, and we all got on like a house on fire. Dad would come home for lunch every day, which I find amazing now. He'd walk from Clery's to Connolly train station, take the train to the first stop, which was Killester, have his lunch, return on the train and be back at work within an hour. Different times.

And thinking of different times, my mother's brother, Michael, who was a Christian Brother and taught in Liverpool, would come home to visit from time to time and my mother would laugh at the memory of my uncle, in full Christian Brother regalia, pushing my pram along the road to the shops, or for a walk. Apparently he loved taking me out in the pram, and why wouldn't he? Sure I was the ideal baby! Michael was quite the character, but he died of a brain haemorrhage before I had a chance to know him, and my grandfather, Mam's dad, also passed away when I was too young to have a memory of him, so there we were, Mam, Dad and me; the Holy Family, my mother called us.* So began the most idyllic childhood

* Do you think she was giving me a Christ complex? Reminds me of a listener's joke: Q: Who invented the fireplace'? A: Alfred the Grate. I'll get me coat.

anyone could hope for. The house was full of love, each for the other, one for all and all for one. When you are young, you just see your parents as Mam and Dad or whatever, but the important thing is the protection that you feel and the love that permeates every day. Well, we had plenty. That's how we were.

They were marvellous at showing an interest in whatever I was about. Mam always had a *grá* for music, cinema and dance. In another world, she would have been a patron of the arts because she enjoyed them all. My dad was happy for us both to have this other side to daily life. He enjoyed it, but wasn't as enthusiastic about it as she was. When they were courting they would go to the Theatre Royal and see the likes of Roy Rogers and Trigger and the other visiting film stars. She also had an autograph book, which sadly I can't find, but I recall her telling me that it contained the signatures of many a fine star of the day. She had her film-star favourites as well: Gregory Peck, David Niven, Richard Burton, Sophia Loren, James Stewart and Robert Donat. All very glamorous. She loved that glamour and I think it sustained her, too, while living a life in suburbia, which was hardly glamorous. Not that she would ever have had aspirations to be on the stage or on the screen, but she loved the stories about them and they were regulars at the cinema.

I clearly remember going to see Norman Wisdom movies with Mam. We adored him. I remember going to see a film of his, *A Stitch in Time*, in 1963. How at the age of seven I was supposed to understand the plot I don't know, but I do recall it was set in a children's hospital and Norman played the part of Norman Pitkin, a hapless butcher's apprentice, who basically caused chaos for the entire film. Then there was *The Early Bird* two years later, when Norman worked for Grimsdale's dairy as a milkman, with predictable results. It's all silly slapstick, but when you're only nine and up to your eyeballs in ice cream and everyone around you is laughing, you get the giggles and it was genuinely funny. The interesting thing is that on radio were getting all this really clever comedy and yet here we were at the cinema and there wasn't really one joke, just a series of mad capers that made you laugh. I suppose you have to work harder on your jokes on radio, where there is nothing visual for the audience to hang on to.

I loved Norman Wisdom from the off and, because we shared a love of his films, it was like a bonding of sorts. Mam was bringing me into her world by introducing me to the cinema. Speaking of Norman Wisdom, years later, I got a call from a man in Baldoyle, who was involved in a vintage car rally over in Terenure College. He wanted someone to act as compère; to introduce the day, to describe the exhibits, the sort of old cars that would be there, to do the raffle and to introduce the special guest … who, over 30 years after I'd first seen him, was only Norman Wisdom. Well, I was like an idiot with the excitement and the first thing I did was call Mam and tell her. She thought this was marvellous and begged me to get his autograph – she hadn't lost that girlish interest in the cinema and those she loved on that screen. As the event drew closer, that fine gentleman in Baldoyle called me and invited Mam and me to have tea with Norman at the gentleman's house. Mam got into a bit of a flap, saying that she had nothing to wear and sure what would he make of her. The Irish mammy was coming out again. When I assured her that he was only three years older than her, it seemed to help, yet it was obvious she was still star struck.

Well, we went and we had tea and cake and chatted; Norman had a kiss for Mam and a little dance. Even at the advanced aged of 89, he still did the Norman Pitkin stumble, his trademark. And we all laughed like it was the first time we'd ever seen it. It was like having John Cleese do the silly walk for you, or Al Pacino go 'Who-haa' as he did in *Scent of a Woman*. Do you know, I actually think she went a little weak at the knees, and her in her dotage herself. This was August 2006 and he was gone four years later at the grand old age of 95, the same age as Mam when she passed seven years later. Norman, we miss you still.

...

The wireless was a big deal in the fifties and into the sixties and was always on in our house. There was Radio Éireann, of course, and Mam also listened to BBC Radio 2, or the Light Programme as it was called then. So, when I was growing up, I had a grounding in Irish radio, but also the delights from the BBC of *Junior Choice*, a programme that played requests from children and children's favourites, as well as the madcap humour of *Beyond Our Ken*, with Kenneth Horne, a sketch show which was the predecessor to *Round the Horne*, and which gave me my first introduction to the genius of Kenneth Williams. On Sundays there was that 'cheeky boy' Jimmy Clitheroe, who was always getting into scrapes in *The Clitheroe Kid*, and my mother could enjoy *Mrs Dale's Diary*, the BBC radio serial about a doctor's wife, just the same as she enjoyed *The Kennedys of Castleross*, Radio Éireann's radio serial. My favourite was *Pick of the Pops*, with its tagline, 'All the hits that fit'. Thanks to Mam, we were immersed in radio and it affected me hugely.

My parents also played a role in my first forays into music. I can't remember my first ever record, but I do remember having a lot of time for Irish acts like Sean Dunphy, Dickie Rock and Val Doonican. So it might have been 'Come Back to Stay', Ireland's Eurovision entry from 1966 or Sean Dunphy with his 'Black and Tan Gun', or, indeed, my party piece, 'Walk Tall', by Val Doonican. That was released in 1964 and I still have the original single.

Now that I remember it, there was a song that I loved from the moment I heard it, and still do, called 'Puff the Magic Dragon' by Peter, Paul and Mary. It was 1963, a year that was to cause great upheaval in the world with the assassination of John F. Kennedy, but back in January, this little song came ambling by. It was very sweet, about an ageless dragon and little boy called Jackie Paper, who eventually grows up and loses interest in the dragon, leaving our fiery friend all alone and quite down. As I tell you this, it doesn't appear at all a nice, child-friendly story, but the music is cute and, until the sad ending, it's a cute story, too. There were suggestions that the song was about smoking marijuana: that 'paper' referred to rolling papers and that the dragon was in fact 'draggin' and the 'puff' self-explanatory. Well, the authors refuted it then and still do. I believe them, I want to believe that there was an innocence to it and the song is too precious to me to have it messed up by dodgy references.* There were other songs I recall from being small: 'Right said Fred', by Bernard Cribbins, 'Lily the Pink', 'The Runaway Train', 'The Ugly Bug Ball', 'Nellie the Elephant', 'Pop Goes the Weasel', 'I Tawt I Taw a Puddy Tat', Dick Van Dyke's 'The Ugly Duckling', and who could forget the song that prepared me for my future years at the Eurovision Song Contest, 'Gilly Gilly Ossenfeffer Katzenellenbogen by the Sea'! This Max Bygraves number was a particular favourite in our house. Even today I still get requests from the listener of a morning for a little bit of Max ... say, 'Wonderful Copenhagen', on the far side of a dose of James Taylor.

Hats off to Mam and Dad, not only did they show me the way, but they knew my interests and let me pursue them and they encouraged them, for which I thank them. In fact,

---

* Now then, a dragon joke. A man dressed in tatty clothes and clearly down on his luck arrives at an inn called the George and Dragon. It's closed but he knocks on the door. The innkeeper's wife puts her head out the window and he says, 'Could you spare me some food?' 'No,' she says. 'Can I have a beer?' 'No,' she replies. 'Can I at least sleep in your barn for the night?' he implores. 'No,' she tells him. 'I'm wondering,' says he, 'Might I have a word with George?'

Mam (with Dad's usual acquiescence, I presume) got me the record player. I'm presuming, based on endless research by me with people much older than me, you understand, that it was a Garrard record player. I'm not talking about something with speakers, this was a mono record player with a turntable and a big plastic lid. Of course, this was bought on the understanding that I would study hard in school – yeah, right. That record player was the beginning of the end as far as school was concerned, my rocky road into how I would spend the rest of my life.

Do you know that Garrard Engineering not only made record players, but were also responsible for the care and maintenance of the British Crown Jewels and the Royal Crown? They made jewellery, gold- and silverware, and not only that, they also manufactured precision rangefinders for artillery. My little record player was but a sideline to these guys, but I loved it with a passion. It had two knobs at the front, one to turn it on that also controlled the volume, as well as another knob that made it trebly if you turned it to the left and bassy to the right. Techno maniacs, we were.

It might be hard to imagine nowadays, when at the touch of a button or the flick of a screen, your favourite tune is downloaded from iTunes, but mine was the era of the 7-inch single, a 'record' that you played on your record player at 45 rpm. One of my early singles was by Paul Jones and the other was an instrumental by Horst Jankowski called 'A Walk in the Black Forest' … imagine walking in a cake. Nonsense. I also remember playing records so much that my great Garrard went on fire, much to the parents' annoyance. They weren't exactly well-off and Dad's wages were far from a princely sum, so I waited for a few paydays to go around before another record player turned up. But turn up it did.*

So, encouraged by Mam, the pop market began to matter to me and the soundtracks to *Mary Poppins* and *The Sound of Music*, as well as the James Bond collection, and artists like Ray Conniff, Nelson Eddy and Jeanette MacDonald, as well as the very popular LP (that's long player in old money) of the hugely successful television show, *The Black and White Minstrels* ... I know, much has been said about this show, but we had no idea at the time how wrong it was – we just liked the music. Interestingly, on a recent Lyric FM trip to Oxford, a colleague and I found a Black and White Minstrels album in Oxfam, which certainly brought us back.

✳ Speaking of records, do you know there is a man who holds the world record for telling the most jokes in one minute: 26 one-liners like, 'My wife and I were happy, then we met,' and, 'I went to the paper shop, but it had blown away.' The reason I think of this is because the jokes sound like Tommy Cooper jokes and my parents loved Tommy Cooper. They also loved Morecambe and Wise and Les Dawson, in fact, all Eric Morecambe had to do was appear on TV and my father would start to laugh. Here is another one a *Marty in the Morning* listener attributes to Tommy Cooper: 'I ate a ploughman's lunch ... he wasn't happy.'

As a youngster, when I'd saved money up for a new album, my mam and I would head into town on the bus to buy it and when I got older, I would make these trips on my own on the number 54a from Killester to town and in to Stan the Man in Dolphin Discs on Talbot Street. It was the beginning of a longstanding relationship with this great man of music. Stan had a happy way about him and always had a warm greeting; he actually got as much satisfaction as we did by having the new releases ahead of any other record shops. When I took to DJ-ing, so many of us went to him for our singles and he would always make sure that our needs were catered for, but my earliest memories of him are with my mam. He had a soft spot for her, too, which endeared him to me.

The price of 28/6 for an LP sticks in my mind. I can still recall the joy of the purchase and the pleasure of coming home on the bus reading every last word on the cover, even down to who printed the blooming thing. I remember it was a crowd in Hayes, Middlesex. For a fella with a crowded mind, I don't know why this image of me upstairs on the bus with the latest LP sticks with me but it does. A moment in time perhaps.

...

So our house was full of music and radio with a nod and a wink to the silver screen. All these things my mam loved and I never once recalled her criticising music that wouldn't have meant anything to her. You were enjoying it, and that was good enough. So when the Monkees arrived in 1966, she never had a bad word to say against them.

At ten, I was hardly ready for the onslaught of the Summer of Love the following year, but the Monkees, now that changed everything. They were shown on RTÉ on a Saturday teatime, just after my bath: I was always spotless when they were on. Davy, Mickey, Mike and Peter ... I loved them with a passion that lasted a good four years. Mam and Dad encouraged me in this, of course, and I remember getting *Sixteen* magazine from America and *Fab 208* and devouring every scrap of information about the band. As fate would have it, some years ago I got to interview Davy Jones and he was as I had hoped, a little gent who, for a time in the sixties, had ruled the airwaves. When I told my mam I was doing the interview she was as thrilled as I was and wanted to know every little detail.

Funny thing was, though, when it came to buying a Monkees shirt, there my parents drew the line. It wasn't every day that a shirt of the magnitude of a Monkees shirt came along, and I begged them for one. Have you ever seen a Monkees shirt? Let me enlighten you. They were worn by the Monkees themselves, and my memory is that they were principally red but also came in blue, with two rows of four white buttons down the front, and three on the cuff. Oh, and I suppose they had winged collars. Do you know what? The simplest thing would be to show you a picture, so here it is.

Now, by the mid-sixties, my dad had already been selling shirts in Clery's for the best part of 15 years. This was a man who knew a shirt, who could tell his poplin from his rayon. He could explain to you in detail about plain weave or twill and about drip-dry and polyester. I remember him regaling us with stories about a shirt you didn't need to iron ... such nonsense, he thought. And yet that last idea certainly put a twinkle in my mother's eye. (It's true, there was an ad on the telly that I recall for Rael Brook shirts; I think a shirt danced on its own in front of a city skyline. My father loved that ad. I think he felt that at last, the shirt had come into its own: in the ad, it had no accompanying trousers.)

Unusually, neither of them wanted to get me the shirt. This hadn't really been the case up to now. All I had needed was for one of them to agree with me about a purchase and the other one would invariably get in line. But on this there seemed to be no shifting them. Ah, yes, I hear you cry. My, what astute parents you had and how wise they were to keep you away from such a garment. My father couldn't be kept away from the offending item, because he passed the shop on Talbot Street where it was for sale four times a day. As it was a glaring red colour he couldn't avoid seeing it. So, would he relent? Would he what.

I wasn't used to this, I have to say, because my parents doted on me, and if I really wanted something, they tried their best to make it happen. One of the perks of being an only child, I suppose. I've often been asked about being an only child and, in particular, the idea of being a 'lonely' only child. I can only speak from my own experience: I never felt loneliness as an only child, because I was under the watchful gaze of my parents at all times. THERE WAS NO ESCAPE!! You see, when you have siblings, you can hide behind them. It's always 'Where's Johnnie?' or 'Jean's late,' or 'Your brother's been a long time at the shops.' When it's only you, they know what time you went out, what time you were due somewhere and what time you said you'd be back. So for an only child it's a bit like living in a police monitoring station: if you're missing for five minutes, a search party will be sent out even if you're only upstairs.

But the other side of that is that, when you get back from the shops, your toys are exactly where you left them, untouched until you decide to play with them again. You don't have a brother who takes your stuff, your socks are all your own and you don't have to share the material things of childhood, like your Dinky/Corgi cars. I had buses, milk lorries, cars of the day, an ice cream car and the great Simon Snorkel fire engine. I would play for hours and hours with my cars, using my imagination, creating stories in my mind based on the driving of cars and trucks, where they went and what they did, having races and adventures and the like. (When you think about it, isn't that all *Top Gear* is? I think I've just discovered why it's been so appealing for so long. People say it's about boys' toys, but the more I think about it, the more the vision of a little boy on the floor with all his cars lined up begins to make sense.) You hear people talk about their toy car collection and its value, but I never kept the boxes, which apparently account for most of the value of the toy; my job, when I got the car home, was to get it out of its box, put the box in the bin and play with the car … the Batmobile, James Bond's Aston Martin DB5 … I even had a Monkeemobile, but I'll come back to that crowd in a bit. I also have a recollection of going to the dentist on occasion and my reward for not screaming the dental surgery down would be a new Dinky/Corgi car. I must have been to the dentist very regularly!*

So I was happy out with my cars, but my parents were particularly conscious of me needing friends. I was lucky to have lots of them on our road. About ten doors down there were the Magees, ten of them, I think. Behind us were the Byrne family; Danny was my best friend for years and I think they numbered about 12. Up the road there was the Grennell family, another ten or so (great basketballers, who played for Killester). Amidst this crowded picture, there were three only boys on the road; Brendan, Liam and me. Anyhow, the point is this, I don't recall being lonely, I recall great friendships, playing up at the park, riding my bike and having a thoroughly enjoyable childhood (apart from my acute inability to study).

* What about the girl who went to the dentist and met an older woman coming out, who said, 'Thank goodness my work is completed. I'm so glad to have found a painless dentist and one who is so gentle and understanding, too.' When the girl was in the dentist's chair, she related the story and the dentist laughed, explaining, 'Oh, that was just my mother.'

When I think about being an only child, I'm often reminded of the song by a man who I don't think has ever really got recognition for the genius of his writings, Jackson Browne. On an album called *The Pretender* he had a song called 'The Only Child'. Talk about hitting the nail on the head; in the song he asks his son to take good care of his mother in life. I didn't know of the tragedy in his life at the time, that his wife had died suddenly in 1976. All I knew was that this was a song written by somebody who clearly understood the only child. The song spoke to me, as they say, because I'd shared that experience.

Some years ago I was in London meeting some people at the BBC (a great line to create havoc in Donnybrook!) and found myself at a loose end at about four in the afternoon. I read up on what was on in London that evening and discovered that the Two Ronnies, Barker and Corbett, were on at the London Palladium. I hightailed it to the box office and was able to get one ticket in a very good location about 12 rows from the front in an aisle seat. That evening I went to comedy heaven, watching two geniuses at work. Lines like, 'The search for the man who terrorises nudist camps with a bacon slicer goes on. Inspector Jones had a tip-off this morning, but hopes to be back on duty tomorrow.' Or, the old chestnut, the 'fork handles' sketch, or genius jokes like, 'We will be talking to a car designer who has crossed Toyota with Quasimodo and come up with the hatchback of Notre Dame.' Wonderful, just wonderful.

I recall heading back to the hotel and having dinner in the restaurant and delving into the bag of goodies I had bought in HMV or wherever at teatime. To my great delight, I had found my favourite film, Alastair Sim and Margaret Rutherford's *The Happiest Days of Your Life*. I was just so happy and so I got on the phone to Maria and told her all about my day. For so many years she has been the first one to be told any good news I have to share and still is. That done, I have a memory of calling my folks as well, sharing the day and wishing them a good night. But the point is, I was fine on my own. Potentially, I suppose that could develop into a sort of selfish attitude in later life but, thank God, I don't do selfish. In fact, I never really did selfish. (And now a completely unrelated line about a shellfish: 'Why wouldn't the shrimp share his treasure? Because he was a little shellfish.' Best told in a Sean Connery accent.)

...

Mam didn't wrap me in cotton wool, but I'd say she was protective, all of which is completely normal, as I was her only child, and I never felt any sense of resentment about it. In her innocence, she didn't really want me to be a boy scout – all that wandering off into the woods – but she was delighted when I became an altar boy. For my sins (don't go there) I became a fully fledged, signed-up member of the altar boy fraternity in Killester parish when I suppose I must have been about eight. I remember being on altar duty at 7.30 a.m. Mass, Monday to Friday, which meant having to be out of the bed, washed and ready for the off at 7.10 (hard on a winter's morning) to run up the street to St Brigid's Church, jump into me soutane and surplice (remembering always the black socks and black plimsolls) to greet the Reverend Father and on to the altar. In those days Masses were said in Latin: *mensa, mensa, mensam*, all of that. Also, we had to say the responses to the priest, also in Latin, because there were probably only about 20 people in the church, usually those closest to the departure lounge. When Communion was being given out, I had to walk beside the priest with the ciborium (a chalice with a lid, for those of you who don't know), and hold an elaborate little tray affair under each communicant in case the host dropped. It doesn't happen today, of course, because people take the host in their hands. Talk about health and safety. Immediately Mass was over, it was back into civvies, dash home, brekkie and school. Cleansed in body and soul and with a full tummy.

Of course, there was Sunday Mass as well and, as one became more senior, one would always be working towards the top of the altar boy hierarchy, when one got to carry the main emblem of the day in front of the procession of Corpus Christi all around the neighbourhood. I think this position was bestowed on me twice, and I can still remember my parents beaming as I passed, as if I'd suddenly been elevated to the position of bishop; somewhere deep down inside, I did indeed feel like a bishop or, at the very least, a monsignor. Bit like the stage really. Whether or not it was preparing me in some ecclesiastical way for *Winning Streak* we'll never know, but it certainly made me realise the importance of washing your face and cleaning your shoes in case anybody might look at you when you'd be out.

But as any fully fledged altar boy (or altar girl) knows, the high points of being an altar server are the big days, Christmas and Easter. They still live in my memory as being incredibly special. Never mind that at Christmas I'd be dragged screaming to Mass, leaving all my lovely presents from Santa behind, to hear about the real meaning of Christmas when I knew full well that the real meaning of Christmas was back home, lying half assembled on the dining-room floor. Yes, I was fully aware of the symbolism of the child in the manger and, indeed, of the animals, the innkeeper, the need to sing 'Joy to the World' and to proclaim the birth of our Saviour, but that Lego wasn't going to make itself and I knew it. I had stickers to put onto my new farm (made of sturdy plastic in a country far removed from the North Pole). But Christmas Mass was and remains hugely important for me, as does Easter, my father's favourite time of year.

The real altar boy nirvana was serving at a wedding. This was full of smiley, happy faces (unless there was some jilting at the altar) and everybody was in good form, but really, it was because we got paid. In the early stages of my wedding serving I just believed all best men were fat when, in fact, it was the bulk of the envelopes that they had to dish out before the party left for the reception that had them in the state they were. Remember, there was none of your credit card nonsense here or transferring to your account; this was proper folding stuff. So the best man would dispense an envelope to the organist, singer, florist, priest, church and, finally, the altar boy – me! This would usually result in a crisp orange 10-bob note, four times my pocket money at the time. In today's money it equates to 50 cents. I hear you cry, 'But that won't make you rich!' Well, let me tell you, four weddings and you had £2. Remember, an LP back then was 28/6, so I could buy an LP and still have over 10 bob left.

...

Where Mam and Dad really came into their own, though, was on the family holiday. In the Whelan household, these were of the traditional type. Dad had his spring week and his autumn week, but in the summer he had the two weeks off. Great plans would be made and conversations would be had about how far the A40 or the Beetle or the Hillman Avenger, whichever we had at the time, would take us. Invariably we ended up going down the east coast, through Wicklow and the Glen of the Downs, through Arklow and Gorey and on to Courtown, our destination for quite a few years. I know that when I was very small, Mam took a trip to Italy with her maiden aunt May from America, the lady who had wanted to adopt her years before, and Dad and I headed off to Courtown. We stayed in the Tara Vie hotel for a week, Dad and I. It has been said, and I presume it's by ne'er-do-wells, that the hotel was in fact called the Tara View, but the W fell off! It's still there over 40 years later and there is no sign of a W. The rest of the time, when it came to the family holidays, it was a caravan for us. I'm not convinced we were caravanning people, but Mam and Dad seemed to think it would add a bit of adventure to the holiday and give us more of an independent air. I suppose it did, because my memories are of sunny days, the three of us taking walks and going down to the beach, building sand-castles, eating sandwiches, and sand in the sandwiches if the slightest bit of wind got up. But my biggest thrill was going to the carnival. I loved the carnival, particularly the chair-o-planes and the dodgems. At the carnival, one of them would take me in the chair-o-plane, usually my dad, and one of them would take me in the bumpers, always my dad. Candy floss would be eaten, my clothes destroyed and then the family would attempt push-penny. We never won a thing, but it didn't matter, we were having fun.*

I always remember the time we went mad for a bit of variety and took a caravan in Arklow. It was the summer of 1969, and I was beginning to crave some freedom, I suppose, because I was turning 13 – eek, a teenager! All was good about the holiday, but the one thing I wanted for my birth-day was a transistor radio. Normally, Mam encouraged whatever interests I had, but this time, she wasn't best pleased and couldn't understand why. She said that it didn't make any sense for me to have my own transistor when the house was full of radios. 'Yes,' said my father quietly and gently, as was his style, 'but now that Martin is 13, he might want to enjoy his own music at his own pace. It's only a

---

* And now a caravan joke ... A policeman pulled over a car and said to the driver, 'Excuse me, but do you know you're driving without a rear light?' The driver jumped out, ran to the back of the car and started to groan. 'Don't take it so hard,' said the policeman sympathetically, 'It's not that serious.' 'Isn't it?' said the driver, 'My caravan's gone.'

push for some freedom, Lil.' He was right, of course, and had the good sense to see it and to respond to it positively. But my mam probably saw it as the beginning of the loosening of her apron strings and my flight to freedom to places like Timbuktu and Melbourne could only be days away. I actually remember that she was quite sad for a little while.

I got the transistor radio and I was beside myself with excitement. (That makes two of me.) I can still see myself walking along listening to the chart show on the radio. I was in seventh heaven. I can still remember the chart of that week with 'Dizzy' by Tommy Roe at number one, followed by the Beatles and 'Get Back', 'My Way' by Frank Sinatra ... then there was 'My Sentimental Friend' from Herman's Hermits 'Oh Happy Day' by the Edwin Hawkins Singers, 'Ragamuffin Man' by Manfred Mann and 'Galveston' from Glen Campbell, another Jimmy Webb composition. That summer also yielded my favourite song of all time, 'Something in the Air' by Thunderclap Newman. Heady times, for the world and for me.

That was also the year my favourite album came out, the Beatles' *Abbey Road* ... It's my favourite bar none. Years later, when Maria and I were in London, we took a picture of ourselves walking across the same pedestrian crossing as the Fab Four on the cover of the album – except when we got there we had to queue up behind a busload of Japanese tourists. When I tried to walk across, I was nearly run over by a London cabbie. Clearly he had seen it all before.

As I grew older, trips to the west of Ireland took place, Bundoran or down to Spiddal, then eventually Mam and Dad were going on holidays on their own, and then, years after that, I was trying to persuade them to come on holidays with Maria and me. Over the years, I tried everything to cajole them to come away, but Dad would use Mam's unwillingness to fly as an excuse. He wouldn't fly either, but never had to admit to it. Mam had a bad experience back in the fifties when she was working for Cassidy's as a buyer, and was on a flight back from London that got stuck in stormy weather over the Irish Sea and she promised God that if she got down safely, she wouldn't fly again. I know it may seem ridiculous – why would God want you not to fly again? – but she made the promise and she stuck by it. It was a huge loss in her life and prevented her from seeing places she would have loved because she had such an enquiring mind: she read voraciously – books and papers – and followed the news all her life.

So one year, when we had been married for a few years, I decided to take my folks on holiday to the UK. We went to Chester, Manchester and Stratford-upon-Avon. At the time, I was driving this lump of a Volvo – it was like an armchair on wheels – and we motored across Wales to Chester with its wonderful black-and-white buildings, and then on to Manchester where the tour of Coronation Street was obligatory, because they watched it religiously, and we also did a tour of Granada Television ('Martin, would you not look for a job here as well?' said Mam). They even had a four-poster bed in the Dominion Hotel on Princess Street in Manchester. They deserved it. The rest of the holiday was spent in Stratford-upon-Avon and it was perfect. We stayed at the Arden Hotel, opposite the RSC. I can still remember our tour of Stratford, where my parents dressed up in costumes from the period of Shakespeare (my father made an intriguing bishop!). We dined at The Shakespeare, of course, sat by the River Avon watching the swans and tried to get my mother to join us on a tour of a butterfly farm, where she nearly had a canary! A canary in a butterfly farm is not a good mix, so we left hastily. We visited all the Shakespeare sites and basically had a ball. It was one of the nicest holidays I ever had, let alone my parents. I felt that I was giving them something back for all the years they had taken me away and it felt so good, and because my parents were of an age when we went, I had to run the show. Running it for them was a joy. Actually, they were hilarious, the two of them. At breakfast in the hotel my mother would stock up on sugar for the room and the little sachets of milk and if the waiter was foolish enough to put those little glass jars of ketchup and mayonnaise on the table, they could kiss them goodbye as well. This wasn't, as my mother would explain, stealing: it was for use on the premises at a later stage.

We went on another trip the following year, to Birmingham and Llandudno, neither of which I have any desire to see again, but it was a chance to be with them alone, not that we needed to rekindle anything, but the idea of the three of us together again on holiday was very special. And even as I tell you this, the memories come flooding back and a warm glow envelops me like a protective blanket. They were such great fun to be with and conversation flowed, but this second trip, in the summer of 1998, proved to be a little step too far for Dad. He wasn't feeling the greatest this time and there were a few occasions where he seemed out of sorts and we had a couple of dazed moments. He'd always had an ulcer problem and, as a lifelong smoker, he wasn't doing himself any favours. (Funnily enough, some of my best times with him were conversations we had at the end of a meal sharing a pack of cigarettes and a glass of something refreshing. He never really drank until I took him under my wing.)

We went home and he went for tests and the news was bad. He was diagnosed with pancreatic cancer. There would be no operation, just time. But how much time? It transpired that he only lasted six weeks and I was absolutely heartbroken. One of our merry band, one of our Musketeers, had ceased to be and the pain at his loss was of a level I had never experienced before. The closest I'd come to death was when Maria's lovely dad Tom had died, far too young at the age of 68, back in 1993, but now my dad was gone at the age of 78. The moment he passed, surrounded by all of us, in his own bed at home, my mam kissed him goodbye and seemed to find an inner strength I had not witnessed in her before.

In the face of the loss of a man she had been married to for 43 years and loved longer, Mam steeled herself for the future. She moved in with us for a while and found a consolation of sorts with us, I hope, but her man was gone and life changed utterly. She lived on in her own home for another 15 years and not a day went by that we didn't speak. She felt better for our nightly phone calls and so did I. She was a part of our lives in a very complete way. She attended every event in our family and extended family: for years she and/or Maria's mum would be with us for the weekend. Some people don't get that, but both Maria and I had that kind of relationship with our parents. We wouldn't accept not being there for them. You owe them that at least.

My mam enjoyed good health all her life and it was really only in her dotage that she required the attention of a geriatrician, which she got in the form of a wonderful man, Mr Dermot Power of the Mater Hospital, as well as Doctors John and Kelly Hanlon and Dr Tony Crosby of Raheny. They all played their part and, without question, made it possible for her to reach her 95th birthday.

Mam came to live with us for the last six months of her life, which was very special, but two Mrs Whelans ended up laid up in separate rooms in our house, when Maria, carrying a duvet downstairs, fell headlong down to the bottom. Our children, relations and friends were simply marvellous and rowed in like the good people they've always been. You can assume all you like, but it's only when help is really required and comes in spades that you know the value of friendship. It meant so much. We feel blessed to have them all in our lives.

One thing's for sure, when your parents are both gone, as are mine, you have a different sense on your shoulders; a new you emerges as you move up the ladder and an awareness grows that you are now an actual adult. Which reminds me, the strangest thing happened at my father's funeral. We had followed his coffin down the church and into the portico at the front, Maria and I minding my mother and our two children, who were only eight and six at the time, and I suddenly turned to nobody in particular and said, 'Where's my dad?' My mind was playing tricks on me – I don't think I had fully understood that he was gone. That's one area where the only child really does stand alone, no matter how close a relationship you have with the love of your life, your life partner, or your children. When you lose a parent as an only child, you are the only person in the world who misses them as a parent. My parents' funerals were, I suppose, the two occasions in my life when I actually felt alone. Perhaps having a brother or sister to share the moment would have somehow eased the pain of the loss at the time; I'll never know. But what I do know is that I was left with the belief my parents passed to me. A belief in oneself at all times, particularly when times are tough, when we are challenged and when a decision to go one way or the other is vital; a belief in the past and holding those memories dear to sustain you when things are not so good; and a belief that those around you who depend on you can have faith in you. The reason my parents were so strong on self-belief, I think, was because they had a sense that, in time, they wouldn't be around and I'd have to stand on my own two feet, alone again, naturally.

...

The weekend before she died, Mam was talking to me about her forthcoming birthday and I asked, 'What would you like, Mam?' Quick as a flash, she replied, 'I was thinking, I'd love a yellow jumper.' This from a woman who had enough jumpers to re-fleece an entire herd of sheep. And what did we do? We bought her the yellow jumper. She never got to wear it. Mam died the day after her 95th birthday. There was great sadness in our family, because we'd lost not just a mother, but a mother-in-law, nanny, friend and confidante. Jessica had just finished a project in college, the Granny Project, a scrapbook chronicle of my Mam's entire life. It is fascinating how Mam kept all manner of memorabilia and how Jessica documented her life and times. We were able to bring it to church on the day of her funeral and display it at lunch afterwards. It brings great comfort even now and I'm very proud to have it.

...

I don't want to end on a sad note here, because Mam and Dad were two fine people who made me the person I am today. Everything they gave me was about positivity, about self-belief, about kindness and understanding towards others and the belief that love is indeed the answer. They were right on all counts and I owe them so much.

'Band on the Run'

Paul McCartney and Wings

I'm not sure where the idea actually came from, but somehow in the middle of secondary school, St Paul's in Raheny, in case you ask, I got this feeling that I wanted to be in a band. I hadn't had much success musically before that time, in primary school in Belgrove NS in Clontarf. Maybe it was down to Mam's love of music, because there was no history of anyone in my family playing an instrument, and as for singing … if you heard my father singing, that would be all the proof you needed that music was not in his blood. My mother used to sing at the top of her voice. I use the term 'singing' in its widest possible sense. I do know that when she sang, the cat tended to look at me quizzically and then hide behind the couch. It's not that the cat didn't realise the great talent my mother possessed, it's just that the sound frightened it to the point where it clearly thought another cat had gotten into the house and somebody was killing it upstairs.*

Which reminds me, all through my formative years we had cats; there was Sooty, the black one, who basically died of old age and being absolutely huge. I'm convinced my parents fed Sooty chocolate, as my memory is that whenever I ate chocolate in the house, the cat would follow me everywhere, but really, it was because of his habit of eating all of our woollen jumpers – talk about having fur balls. After that, along came Pinky, a white cat. (I know you're asking the same question I'm now asking: 'Why didn't you call the cat Whitey?') Pinky lived for a few years with us and then just decided to shag off. He was closely followed by the arrival of Oscar, another white cat. Now, Oscar was the most wonderful pet; attentive, affectionate, strangely thoughtful for a cat, a purrfect cat. In fact, Oscar was everything you'd want in a dog without actually being a dog. But there was a strange fact about Oscar; this cat was, in fact, a girl! In all my years in show business I have never met a girl called Oscar … Perhaps I'm not hanging around the right area of show business for this to occur but, nonetheless, having a female cat called Oscar was something we kept to ourselves.

* We often hear from Eileen the Wonder Cat on the wireless of a morning; in fact she sent me this the other day: What did one earthquake say to the other? 'It's not my fault!' Clever cat, Eileen.

In spite of Mam and Dad's singing abilities, I had had music in my life even before my age reached double digits, so it was probably inevitable that I would do something that involved music. My folks decided the one thing I needed to do was learn an instrument, so a piano teacher was employed. I can't recall why we had a piano in the house but we did and the only person who ever played it was my Auntie Kay, my dad's sister. The great thing about my Auntie Kay was that she only knew one tune: the tune she could play, play well mark you, was called 'Chopsticks'. For those who need to know, it was written by Euphemia Allen under the pseudonym Arthur de Lulli and is also known, if you have a German bent, as 'Der Flohwalzer'. Sounds like something from a carnival.

Anyway, whenever she called to the house, that was her tune. She would try to inveigle me to play along with her and attempted to teach it to me and I must've made some fist of it because piano lessons were arranged. The poor woman who came to teach me was up to her eyeballs in Brahms and Liszt, not forgetting Mozart and Tchaikovsky. The problem for me was that I wanted to play Val Doonican and the Monkees and maybe a bit of Sean Dunphy for variety. So clearly this was going nowhere fast. The poor woman trudged to our house every Thursday for my hour's lesson and I just couldn't get it, I think because I didn't want to get it. So that stopped.

Then came the guitar lessons with my best friend from school, Leo Conway. Both of us went to the guitar aficionado, nay,

maestro, Norman Teeling in Clontarf. Not only was he a
fine guitar player, but also an artist of some renown and a
former Mr Universe, so you didn't argue with him. He was
a great teacher and we both learned well, Leo mastering
the style of Carlos Santana and me, well, more Jimmy
Santana, his far less accomplished brother. Hang on a
second, now that I think of it, we went on to enter a talent
show in St Paul's one Christmas and came second with our
rendition of Simon and Garfunkel's 'The Sound of Silence'.
We were pleased to be placed in the top three but a bit put
out by the fact that the winners were a five-piece band who
mimed to the Rolling Stones' 'Paint it Black'. After all, our
fingers had bled for our art.

I've always had natural rhythm and strumming the old
guitar was no bother at all, but something made me
change. One of my friends Donal (Doish) had a brother
Gary and he was a great drummer. I used to get behind his
set of drums from time to time and loved it; I seemed to
have a natural aptitude for it. Or maybe it was just about
making noise, which reminds me of a joke: little Johnny
says to his mammy, 'I want to be a drummer when I grow
up,' and his mammy says, 'But, Johnny, you can't do both.'
Okay, enough already!

So, I started to play the drums and I'd basically beg, borrow
or steal a kit to play, but eventually my folks bought me a
set for £25, a princely sum at the time and no mistake. But
that was typical of my parents; if I saw a path that I felt
was right for me, sure they'd ask all manner of questions

about it, but once convinced, they would do everything to help me. My dad would always be the more sceptical: he needed a bit of bringing around, but with Mam it was different. If I told her I was interested in something, she would support me pretty quickly. But of course, the drums were bought on the basis that it was only a hobby.

When I think back on my drumming years, I think it was Norman Teeling who told me that I had great rhythm but as for the guitar, 'You're not great at the chords, because you require the forefinger on your left hand to go across the fret board.' Or words to that effect, whereas Leo had mastered every chord under the sun. I actually do recall him saying that if he could put the two of us together, Leo and myself, we'd make one hell of a guitarist.

However, being able to play the drums in secondary school got me into Sing Out! Now, this will need some explanation. This organisation was created in 1950, apparently to 'preserve and support the cultural diversity and heritage of all traditional and contemporary folk musics, and to encourage making folk music a part of our everyday lives'. I got this explanation from their website, so it must be so. The songs we performed were by people like Woody Guthrie, Pete Seeger, Phil Oakes and Lead Belly, but it was also about religious harmony. My memory of it is that we also featured songs like, 'What Colour is God's Skin?' I can remember it to this day, not the colour, the song. Here we go:

What colour is God's skin,
What colour is God's skin,
I said, it's black, brown, it's yellow, it's red
    and it is white,
Everyone's the same in the good Lord's sight.

And you think I learnt nothing in school. Sing Out! was the idea of Father Joseph McCann, one of the finest Vincentians I've come across. Now, marry this idea with another organisation we were members of in school: Up with People. This particular organisation was about 'bridging cultural barriers and creating global understanding through service' and, wait for it, a musical show. It is all beginning to sound like the Eurovision Song Contest, worryingly so. The main song goes:

Up, up with people, you meet them wherever
    you go,
Up, up with people, they are the best kind of
    folks we know,
If more people were for people then we know
    that everywhere,
There'd be a lot less people to worry about and
    a lot more people who care.

Yes, I know you're sitting there with your cynical hat on but, in fact, it's not the worst sentiment in the world by any means, particularly in the world we inhabit right now. But look, I was in the band on the drums, and our lads from St Paul's in Raheny, my alma mater, were singing their hearts out. But there is an element to this I haven't mentioned yet: St Paul's Boys' College teamed up with the Manor House girls of Raheny in this endeavour. I salute you, St Paul's. I don't know what it did for my drumming, but at least I had the chance, along with all the other lads, to engage with the ladies of Manor House school in a musical way. Indeed.

Actually it was at St Paul's that they gave us the use of a room to practise in, because we could be quite loud. Around Killester, Raheny and Clontarf at this time there must've been half a dozen bands and I'm sure the same story was replicated all over Dublin. Little did we know, in 1973 and 1974, that two years later, in 1976, Larry Mullen Jr would post a message on the Mount Temple Comprehensive School noticeboard looking for fellow schoolmates to join a band. Or that subsequently they would become the biggest band ever to come out of Ireland and among the biggest acts ever in the world. Even at this remove, they were never in any danger of being outshone by us.

We were actually a rock band and there were four of us: Donal Nagle on guitar, Shay Cafferkey on bass, Dermot O'Sullivan on keyboards and yours truly on drums. I guess I should probably tell you the name of the band. Without any airs or graces, without even the slightest hint of pretension, we called the band Ulysses. Before you start going on about it, we based the name not on Greek literature, but on James Joyce's book of 1922 about the exploits of Leopold Bloom on one day in Dublin. So all we were doing was expressing our Dublinness. Hang about, what about our heroes, U2, who called themselves after the World War Two spy plane? Frankly, they can do no wrong in my eyes because what they did was fulfil their dreams and become the biggest band in the world. But we did the exact opposite, fair play to us.

I suppose it's funny when I look back on it now, but we had two major flaws in our band: one, we had no lead singer and two we couldn't write songs for nuts. You can see this wasn't going to end well. Boy, could we whack out the hits, songs like 'All Right Now' by Free; Deep Purple, Uriah Heep, Black Sabbath, Wishbone Ash, Jethro Tull and Pink Floyd. Are you getting the impression that we were a little overambitious? St Paul's College put on concerts and we had already seen fine Irish bands like Alyce, Elmer Fudd and the wonderful Thin Lizzie so we knew what worked. Also, we seemed to do an inordinate amount of practising to the point where we should have been brilliant – I suppose in our own minds we knew we were pretty good, but were we going to set the world on fire?

I remember a number of gigs we played and I can't for the life of me remember how we got them. We played support to a band from Limerick called Reform at UCD and, during our set, we went through the entire side two of Pink Floyd's 1971 album *Meddle*. I remember in particular a track called 'Echoes'. If my memory serves me correctly, it lasts about 10 minutes and I'm sure many a student slipped home for a cup of tea with their parents during our rendition and returned to find us still playing the same song. Very heady stuff. We also played support out at Red Island in Skerries, a rocky headland indeed, but also home to a holiday camp, to the great Horslips. The Celtic rockers were a huge act at the time. I've always contended that they ensured that their amps would only go so high so that when they came on, they would sound like a train emerging from a tunnel, while we sounded like a transistor radio. Years later, I worked with Jim Lockhart from Horslips, now a radio producer, and he absolutely denied such a possibility ... yet his smiling face made me think otherwise. I'm still convinced of it, though I'll never prove it.

I also remember another night that involved my poor Dad. Before I tell you this, we need a joke here to cheer us up. James O'Connor of our listening crew in the morning told me about an LP he bought, which was made for the German market and featured the late, great musician Derek Bell, he of the Chieftains. Apparently the Germans entitled the album: *Derek Bell Plays with Himself*. A bit of humour there for music aficionados.

Well, because I couldn't drive at that stage, my poor father had to transport me and my drums to whatever gig we were playing. I think he was driving an Austin A40 at the time, not spacious. We had this gig to play in a venue in Dublin city centre run by Pat Egan, a legend in musical circles, called the Osibisa (the name of a band at the time) on South King Street, opposite the Gaiety Theatre. Pat Egan is one of life's true gentlemen, then and now. He ran the Sound Cellar record shop in a basement on Nassau Street and I remember buying Santana's *Caravanserai* there, and many more, including, funnily enough, Osibisa! He's a cool guy, always was, and I like him enormously. Anyway, that night we were to play from 10 to midnight for £8. This we duly did except that there was nobody in the place. A bit of a Derek Bell moment actually, so Pat suggested that it would be best if we started our set again at midnight and played until 2 a.m.! I went out to tell my dad the good news and he did what was typical of him: he fumed silently. But wait he did, the poor man, and when we eventually finished at 2 a.m., we noticed that we still got paid the original £8. The innocence of it all from this remove. But that's the way of it when you're trying to make your name.

I also played with a wedding band from time to time, but that was only when there were weddings on ... But our little band really got nowhere. The rest of the lads had a mind to take it seriously, but by this stage, I had started out in the PMPA, that fine insurance company, after leaving school, and certainly couldn't have committed to any sort of permanent situation. So, I kept hesitating and hesitating and I think I just ran out of road really: when the band played a gig in Clontarf with Gary on the drums, replacing me, I felt my lack of commitment was beginning to have an effect on them. I couldn't give the time or the commitment they needed, so, after a small number of appearances, and nothing much to show for it, that was that for me.

Could it have amounted to anything? Hard to say, except that Donal, one of the most handsome men on the Northside, Shay and Dermot were all genuinely good musicians, and if any of us could have written at least one song something could have happened, but it wasn't to be. Anyway, by that stage, I'd met Maria – I was in love, or had you forgotten – and I was ready to head down a different road, about which more later.

...

When I stopped playing the drums in the mid-seventies, I never did play them again, at least not in the same way. It was as if they had been part of a particular stage in my life and were gone. From time to time I'd wonder what it would be like to play again, but just didn't. At least, not until years later when I took over as RTÉ commentator for the Eurovision Song Contest in 2000. (I had commentated on the 1987 Eurovision Song Contest, when Johnny Logan won for the second time, but I'll fill you in on that later.) Back then there was no thought of two semi-finals before the final, so we had a little space to enjoy ourselves in the Euro Club, a spot where the talent from all over Europe descends and everyone just performs with a house band. Great fun. That year our representative in the Eurovision was Eamonn Toal, with a song called 'Millennium of Love', and we came sixth, by the way. Anyhoo, one night in the Euro Club, Eamonn was singing up a storm and he knew that once upon a time I had played the drums. So I got asked up to play while he gave them a rendition of 'Sweet Home Alabama', the old Lynyrd Skynyrd classic. I actually got away with it and my current wife was there to see it (that's Maria, in case you're curious) as well as our head of delegation, my friend Kevin Lenihan. Funnily enough, he never suggested I should take up the drums in a professional capacity. A wise man!

...

I suppose when I look back at my foray into the musical world as a player, I realise that I was never really going to go for it. It's probably to do with commitment. Because without real commitment, very little happens in your life. From time to time you have to fight the brickbats and move on, but you do so because you believe in your capability in whatever you're doing. This 'drumming business', as my folks used to call it, took a real force of will to succeed at and my mind was caught between starting a career, being in love with Maria and being really not sure which direction to go. So, the drumming career came to nought. Do I regret it? Actually, no, because I never really felt in charge of it, never really felt the career was beckoning in this regard. And if you don't feel that, then you need to do something else.

For me, that 'something else' was to lead me to radio. I'd started working in PMPA after leaving school – in those days, that was the way: the bank or insurance if you weren't going to college. I remember I used to walk up and down the public office in my suit asking the great public if they had an 'anti-jacknifing device' – fortunate, because they'd get a discount if they did. However, I knew that if I wanted to progress, I'd have to do exams and take it seriously and I felt it wasn't for me. Now, I had a friend in PMPA, Michael Cotter, who knew that I had a big record collection and who invited me to come over to Radio Dublin, one of the first pirate radio stations in the country, based in the front room of a house in Inchicore, to try my hand at DJ-ing. And so, off I went and did a bit of this and a bit of that – a soul show on a Sunday afternoon and an oldie show at teatime – all for nothing, just because I loved doing it. I suppose I was fortunate in that I came in at the birth of pirate radio and, after Radio Dublin, I went to work at another station called Big D, run by James Dillon. Dave Fanning was at the station, as was Gerry Ryan, and I did a drivetime show there, thanks to my manager at PMPA, Mr Giles, who would give me half an hour off to head to Chapel Lane. I was never paid a penny, because it was all about learning my trade, and I went by the jaunty name of Marty Hall at the time: lest you misunderstand, taking a 'stage' name was the way things were done, and I was a big fan of Hall and Oates ...

...

I have no regrets about not 'making it' as a drummer. When you hear stories of bands on the road up and down the country in a Transit van trying to make a living, you realise how hard it is to be in a band. Of course, the glamour of the few who actually make it and particularly those who make it big, can blind you to the actuality of the life. Look at *The X Factor* or *The Voice* and how difficult it is to make it to the final selection, let alone win.

(What my old piano teacher would make of it all is beyond understanding.) Look at the thousands who constantly turn up for the auditions and never even make it onto the show. The number of broken hearts is unimaginable and desperately cruel. Apart from anything else you don't see many drummers on *X Factor*! Which reminds me of a joke: an amateur drummer died and went to heaven. He was waiting outside the pearly gates and could hear the finest drumming he'd ever heard. He recognised the playing and asked St Peter if that was Buddy Rich (only the finest drummer who ever lived, in my estimation). St Peter replied, 'No, that's God. He just thinks he's Buddy Rich.' On a more serious note, I suppose it's why I feel that anything we can do for musicians when they come in to us for interviews or to play, we should do. The life is hard and uncertain, and with shows like *The X Factor* and *The Voice*, it's particularly hard for certain musicians, like garage bands or singer-songwriters, to be heard, so I always feel it's appropriate to give them time to tell their story and find out how they got to where they are, because so many don't get that opportunity. Perseverance is a great man, but just because you try and try again doesn't mean you have any guarantee of success. Those who achieve it, we must applaud, and those who strive without success, we must also applaud for trying. The world turns, things change and how things are done changes. Yet some things are not for changing, things like family, concern, love, looking out for each other, being there for each other.

...

For many years, any time that I would do an interview when I was becoming known through radio and television, the interviewer would be aware that I had played in a band when I was in school and would ask me about it. My mother would read this and rail against it: 'You never played in a band, son, sure you didn't?' To which I would reply: 'Yes, when I was in school and starting to work in insurance.' 'Well,' she'd reply, 'that's not really playing in a band.' I suppose because it wasn't professional she deemed it some sort of hobby. She was very put out that anyone should think I was doing it professionally. Mad really, but it does remind me of the lovely present she gave me for my 50th birthday. Even though my professional drumming days were behind me, I'd often hankered after having a set so I could play along with some songs whenever the mood took me. So, one day, just before my birthday, Mam said to me, 'From time to time you mention the drums and I was thinking, as I bought your first set, I'd like to buy you your last set.' I was dumbstruck (a rarity); the fact that she felt this way was one thing but that she wanted to act upon it quite another. I was so proud of her that she felt this way and wanted to close the circle. She presented me with a set of Premier drums, with two floating toms and set of cymbals to boot. I am now ready to be pressed into service whenever a passing band needs a drummer. Give me half an hour to get me rhythm back and we're all set.

'When Will I See You Again'

The Three Degrees/Stylistics

Here's a good one for you. I met my wife, Maria, at the Grove hop in Clontarf. I don't know what she was doing there … Clearly she wasn't my wife at the time but I decided as soon as I set eyes on her that she was the one. I know people talk about love at first sight all the time and some people scoff at the very idea – well, I'm living proof that it happens and that it works. Now, I add a word of caution here: it wasn't a two-way street. The amount of wooing I had to do over the following years would have worn out lesser men. But that night under the heady lights of the Grove on a balmy evening in early August (the 7th, actually) 1974, I was on fire! Funnily enough, though there was obviously passion on my mind, I was a nervous wreck. I know, you look at me today, oozing confidence from every pore and striding manfully on, but back in 1974, I was a different kettle of fish. I had no idea how to talk to girls. Maybe it was because I was an only child, not having a sister to talk to about the girly stuff. I always thought it would have been great to have an older sister, someone to confide in, someone to talk to about girls and so on, but maybe I'm idealising things. I talk to friends who have older sisters and they tell me that, in their teenage years, they hardly spoke to each other.

Meantime, back to the Grove and my absolute and utter determination to ask this girl up to dance. She appeared to be dancing with her friend at the time so that meant that at least she was mobile. Leave it to me to set my sights on a moving target.* Cecil the DJ played whatever he played, probably a popular waxing of the day by Slade or some-body and then ... time for me to begin the perspiration (no panic, I had applied the Brut deodorant earlier in the evening). So the first song ended, and then it was on to the second one, the third ... and not a move from your hero. My legs remained rooted to the spot as though they were weighed down with bricks. Now, two of the bouncers,

---

*   Cecil the DJ was always the Grove DJ. He had a soft, unassuming air, but possessed a wealth of knowledge about music and a natural flair for making every night at the Grove go like a dream. A man of impeccable taste and variety, blending Bob Dylan's 'Positively Fourth Street', 'Jean Genie', Pink Floyd's 'Us and Them', Leonard Cohen and the very best of the charts at the time. A perfect blend for the varied ages at the Grove. As I think of it, more of an influence on my tastes than I'd at first realised.

Gerry and Denny, were aware of my intentions, as was Cecil, and now all eyes were upon me, urging me to ask the future mother of my children up to dance. By this stage, the hop had turned into one giant slow set. (I think it was song number six, when they realised that the sales of fizzy drinks had begun to taper off, that there was panic all round by the management.)

So I made my move and actually asked her up. She said yes and that was that. The lads all smiled and nodded in approval and I wanted the moment never to stop. I remember the song too, we both do: ' Ruby Tuesday' by Melanie. But end it did and back this girl, who I learned was called Maria, went to her pal and me to my lot, with my heart all a flutter. At that moment I just knew, without any hesitation whatsoever, that this was the girl for me, and so it proved. (Which reminds me of a joke about the fellow who asked a girl if she'd like to dance and when she replied that she would, he said, 'Good, can I take your chair?')

Anyhow, the Grove opened on a Wednesday in the summertime, so off I went the following week and there she was and without much hesitation, well, the time it took to drink a bottle of Coke, I asked again and she said yes and thus began the next 40 years of my life. When we met – now you must remember it was the mid-seventies – I sported a far-too-tight red shirt, while Maria favoured a green skirt; why I remember this, I'll never know, but I am happy to report that neither of us possesses items like these any more. Far too stylish for the likes of that now.

But I knew that Maria would make the world a better place and I wanted to be beside her for the trip. I felt that connection to her immediately: it took her a bit longer – but she was, and is, warm, caring and just a giving person. She's in my corner constantly, which really matters in this business, which has its ups and downs, and because we started out with nothing, and we started out together, this makes us very grounded.

When I met Maria at the Grove, I had just left school, but Maria had one year to go, so she returned to school for her final year and I started a job in PMPA, where I remained for five years. Our courtship was typical of the time, I suppose: with me working Monday to Friday and Maria getting to grips with the Leaving we really only saw each other at the weekend and in a way that made it more exciting. This was in the time before mobile phones; so my phone calls to her house were fairly obvious; as an only child, I had access to the old phone, but not so the future Mrs Whelan. Maria has a sister, Karen, and four brothers, David, Thomas, Aidan and Gary, and with the one phone in the hall, all and sundry would have a chance to listen in. We got through and survived on those phone calls and letters and cards, and seeing each other at the weekends.

Music played a huge part in our lives. I could give you a list of all our favourite songs in the period but, quite rightly, I think I'll leave that be. Okay then, you asked for it; ABBA and 'Waterloo', the Chi-Lites and 'Homely Girl', John Denver with 'Annie's Song', Paul McCartney with

'Band on the Run', the Stylistics and 'You Make me Feel Brand New', as well as Barry White, the Walrus of Love, and 'You're the First, the Last, my Everything'. But the song that seemed just right for us was the big summer hit that year; the Three Degrees and 'When Will I See You Again'. I hear its opening strains and, suddenly, it's 1974.

My efforts to woo Maria were sterling. I took her to our first ever concert, to the Stylistics. Back in those days, we really didn't have the venues to attract the big acts, apart from the National Stadium. So when someone had the bright idea of bringing the Stylistics to Ireland they thought to themselves, here's one of the biggest acts in the world (as they were then), so let's put them on outdoors in the RDS jumping arena and bring them in on a horse-drawn carriage. All very regal and lovely. This they did and then performed for about an hour, much to the annoyance of the crowd. Maria and I were only young and hadn't a bob and so we were incensed at the end of it, to the point where I even wrote to *New Spotlight*, a music magazine, to complain, which was most unlike me.

I also remember a time when I took Maria out to dinner at Clontarf Castle in what was clearly another effort to impress her. We were having our dinner and I noticed some black stuff at the bottom of our wine bottle and I thought to myself, this is a rum do. Imagine – a lovely spot like this and there's gunk at the bottom of the bottle. I called the waiter over to complain and guess what? Rather than make it clear that there was sediment in the bottle because the wine was half decent, he very kindly replaced it with a different bottle. I wouldn't mind, but I don't think I can afford wine *with* sediment these days.

From the very earliest stages of our relationship, if we had a few bob, we tended to go out together for a meal. We love going to dinner and having the chat. In fact, we've never lost that sense of conversation, that constant sharing of thoughts and ideas and whatever. We used to love a bistro on Baggot Street, Kilmartin's. Best cannelloni in Dublin. Sadly gone. Now, our favourite spot is the Trocadero, and our favourite man, the maître d', Robert Doggett. Whenever we have had a major event in our lives, we have gone to the Troc. Birthdays, anniversaries, losses, successes, reunions, communions, confirmations, whatever … it's the Trocadero. Maître d' Robert has always been the finest host and welcomes us even when it's full. We are friends, and on more than one New Year's Eve, we have made our way home happily from the Troc as brightness fills the first day of the New Year. Robert has an excellent sense of style and the place holds so many memories for us. We've laughed and cried on its crushed velvet banquettes and it's a place of great warmth whenever we're there. They even have a photo of me as a boy broadcaster on the wall.

But I digress. The seventies was an interesting time to grow up in and we were discovering a new world for us to inhabit as a couple. Lots of things were happening in the world, like the end of the Vietnam War, the renaissance in movies, with *The French Connection, The Godfather, The Deer Hunter*

... and let's not forget the first president to resign in office, Richard Nixon in August 1974, the month I met Maria. I found someone and at the time he lost nearly everything.

Meeting Maria's parents for the first time was quite the moment. It was her debs and we had been together a year by that stage. I had gotten my hair cut in town that day, somewhere on Mary Street, so as to impress with an international hairstyle. It was certainly that – more Igor than I'd imagined, and if Hammer Films had been passing and on the lookout for a ghoul's helper I was definitely your man. But it must have gone okay; they didn't turn me away. Tom was strict and always stayed up, reading every inch of the paper, until I deposited Maria home, and we were never later than 2 a.m. No question of a night or a weekend away. As time passed we all got on so well and enjoyed many lively chats at Maria's with her dad. We all became very close as the years passed.

I remember when Maria and I would go for our Sunday drives we would often have a chaperone. How? Well, the baby of the family and Maria's little sister Karen (only nine when we met) was our chaperone. She would wave us off from her bedroom window when we left and then two minutes down the road we'd feel sorry for her and go back and bring her with us on our day out to Bray or wherever. Her mum always referred to her as careless and gay – which she certainly was. But she's turned out to be my favourite sister-in-law – the only one, actually – and we're very close, and she has become a marvellous friend. In fact, she was one of the finest when my mam was in need of anything in her own home, and subsequently when she was ill Karen was a constant; love her so. Now she has her own gorgeous family, Caoimhe, Clara and my brother-in-law John, who, like myself, is partial to the odd bit of 'soup'.

Meantime, our relationship was blossoming nicely. I was getting used to the idea of being invited over to Maria's house for tea at this stage. As an only child, I'd never had to fight for the bit of bread, but, even though there was always a very fine table set in Maria's house, there were eight of them compared to our three. My God, or *mon Dieu*, as they say in France. The other thing that amazed me was the amount of badinage that was going on at the table – this really has an international flavour, doesn't it? In my house it was a much more sedate affair. With three plates of food, you knew where you were, but I found myself number nine at the Dent sitting (that's the current wife's maiden name, always the exotic side of our relationship). I needn't tell you, it was all a bit of a shock. They would have the bants about where someone had been or who wanted the last piece of chicken or anything at all, actually: it was the sheer amount of chat that went on at the table that amazed me. Sure, at home with Mam and Dad I always had the chat, but it seemed more ordered somehow; this was chat on a mega scale. As the years passed and I got more used to it, I was well able to hold my own, but it wouldn't always work and I'd find myself going a bit quiet again.

The one thing that always got the banter going at the table was the sharing out of sherry trifle. Now, you may think

Nana Whelan, Aunty Rita
cousins Anne and Paul.

In the pram on an
outing – 6 months.

Nana and Aunty
Kay directing
me in my car.

Party for one.

Always driv

In a duffle coat,
before they
were trendy.

Is that a camera?

With Nana Whelan, Aunty Kay, Aunty Rita and Mam on my communion day.

With Mam and
our spoiled cat

Mam and Dad on a posh
Courtown holiday.

ON THE AIR

Boy broadcaster.

CLIFF RICHARD

Norman Teeling captures the DJ.

— NORMAN Teelin 1989

Machu Picchu in Peru with our oldest friends, Pauline and Pat.

Bob Geldof drops by – tanned or what?

Radio Telefís Éireann
Marty Whelan
Presenter
Radio/
Television

My friend and producer Ian McGarry helping Phil Collins hold up his gold discs.

Chris Rea, one of my favourites. (© *RTÉ Stills Library*)

At Wham's final concert at Wembley, London.

Our wedding day,
13 August 1985.

Apart from VIP
Most Stylish Man,
my only award.

Jacob's RADIO &
TELEVISION
AWARDS '86

PRESENTATION ON 5TH JUNE 1987
AT THE BURLINGTON HOTEL, DUBLIN.

Our Jessica, days old.

Head to Toe on TV – Fran Duff and my friend Mary O'Sullivan. (© *RTÉ Stills Library*)

Feeding baby Thomas.

The legend Kenny Everett

With Maxi at the National Song Contest. (© *RTÉ Stills Library*)

...ad and I attempt to ...old on to Thomas, ...o's wearing my 1st ...irthday suit on his 1st birthday.

A wheat field on the way to Co. Down.

A hero – Spike Milligan.
(© *RTÉ Stills Library*)

RTE invites you to a

"Marty Party"

to launch the new TV Music and Chat Show

"Off the Record"

Date:	Wednesday 15 September
Time:	6.00 - 8.00 p.m.
Venue:	Gandon Suite South
Davenport Hotel
Merrion Square
Dublin 2.

First Transmission Date
**Sunday, 19 September,
9.20 p.m., RTE 1**

R.S.V.P.
Pauline Bracken,
Press Office, RTE
Telephone (01) 642321 / 643434

Monkee and
eán O'Riada,
mixing it.

Interviewing John
Hume, my Irish hero.
(© *RTÉ Stills Library*)

Mam and Dad do the nightlife.

With Dad on a night out.

Big Chris Roche, the brother I never had.

My pride and joy.

Mam at the Butterfly Farm in Stratford-upon-Avon.

Dressing up.

Our dinner table –
three generations.

you've had sherry trifle, but can I just tell you this, unless the sherry trifle you had was made by Kathleen Dent, then you haven't had sherry trifle. Here's the secret ingredient: Kathleen didn't drink, never did, and as a result, she had a heavy hand. You know, some things in life are really a blessing. Kathleen's sherry trifle was made in heaven. In fact, as I got more and more used to them and they to me, Maria's dad Tom and her brother Thomas and I would fight happily over seconds. In the fullness of time and in the interests of fairness, all three of us got seconds and I think that's where my relationship with the family began to cement itself. Cemented by sherry trifle and, of course, the fact that I was a lovely fella, but then you were clearly in no doubt about that.*

I mentioned the cinema earlier, and going to the pictures has always been a very important part of any courtship, as it was for ours. It was about the picture, yes, it was about eating ridiculous snacks in the dark, yes, but let's face it, it was really about being together in the dark. Any questions? Good, then I shall proceed. Going to the pictures in the late seventies and early eighties was very different from today. First, you couldn't book on the phone and, second, you didn't have a credit card anyway, so it was into town on the bus. Most places had a local cinema then, but it was literally one cinema, and Dublin city offered you the incredible choice of four cinemas: the

---

✱ Speaking of food, Joe Gantly of our morning gathering on the wireless tells me some exciting news that explorers in Egypt's Valley of the Kings have discovered a body completely covered in chocolate and nuts; they think it may be the tomb of Pharaoh Rocher!

Savoy, the Carlton across the road and, down in Middle Abbey Street, the Adelphi, and the Ambassador on Parnell Street. So Maria and I would get on the bus and go into town to experience the joy of joining a queue. Now, Saturday night and Wednesday night were the big nights, so we queued and queued … I'm talking about a queue that snaked from the front of the Savoy down around the corner into Findlater Street. There was a certain inevitability to the whole scenario: we'd queue, getting closer and closer, having paid off the couple of buskers that came along and poor Mary, an O'Connell Street character, who was a legend among cinemagoers, and the chances were that the cinema would be full with about 14 people ahead of you. You'd spent all this time queueing to be with your girlfriend and enjoy the delights of, say, *Grease* or *Midnight Express* or *Revenge of the Pink Panther* or the dancing joy of *Thank God It's Friday* and, suddenly, the hairy hand would go up and say, 'That's it. We're full.'

I was always at a loss as to what to do when this happened. There was always the Carlton cinema across the road but they had very hard seats, not at all conducive to minding the girlfriend in a comfortable manner. But we were out, so we had to go to something. Maybe we'd take a stroll down Middle Abbey Street towards the Adelphi to see what delights they'd have: a steely determination meant that you would go to practically anything just to be together. Do we sound desperate? I think everybody was the same. I remember once Maria noticed that *Gone with the Wind* was playing at the Ambassador and decided that it would be marvellous to see such a classic on the big screen. I did my,

'Of course, love, what a great idea,' routine and promptly fell asleep for a good hour during the movie. I'm not convinced I missed anything. After all, I knew Rhett Butler wouldn't give a damn if I watched all of it or not.

The other thing that was quite popular was the drive on a Sunday. Do couples still go for that? We did the odd trip to Dalkey or Greystones as a day-long adventure, really, just an aimless drive, a change of scenery and a bit of a day out. Now, in the early stages of our courtship, we had no car so that did tend to put the idea of the drive in some sort of jeopardy. I had access to my dad's VW Beetle, never a great car for a quick, or, indeed, quiet, getaway, but it did the job and gave us the beginnings of freedom and my folks were very giving with it. In the early days, I had to get two buses from Killester to Beaumont, where Maria lived, but, as I was working away in the PMPA, in time, the car loan happened. Up to that stage I was able to blame the buses for the fact that I was, frankly, always late. How Maria put up with me in those early days, I'll never know. I seemed to find it possible to leave home at the time I was due to arrive somewhere else.* Incidentally, I was late for our second date as well, and Maria waited, and now, it seems, it's my turn to wait ... in perpetuity.

* Which reminds me of the joke about the girl who waited over an hour for her date and then decided she'd been stood up. She went home, took off her frock and got into the jammies and settled down with a pizza in front of the TV. There was a knock at the door and who should it be but her date: 'Good heavens, I'm a couple of hours late, and you're still not ready?'

Thanks to the PMPA and the car loan, I got myself my very first car, a Datsun 100A. What a car it was: bright yellow and as thin in the bodywork as a slice of Denny ham. It was also called a Datsun Cherry and the colour was described as 'sunny yellow'. I thought I was the bee's knees; in fact, if I wore something black driving my yellow car, I *was* the bee's knees. We were thrilled with ourselves, Maria and me; suddenly the world was our oyster. There's nothing like that freedom that comes with a first car and the feeling that you can suddenly go anywhere, night or day. I do remember Mam suggesting that I get covers for the seats though, which reminded me of a neighbour we had who'd covered his seats in transparent plastic to keep them clean. Imagine what that would have been like on a hot day, as you'd slide off onto the floor!

Off we went in our little yellow car, a Sunday afternoon drive here, a picnic there … a crash … My first actual car crash happened outside Belton's pub in Donnycarney on an icy road. In an effort to avoid an oncoming bus, I'd decided to slam on the brakes, but accidentally floored the accelerator and ended up crashed into a parked car. Nice one, Mart. Thankfully, nothing and nobody was hurt except my pride; I'm pretty sure that's the only incident we had.*

✳ And here's another one from a *Marty in the Morning* listener: Johnny was driving down the road and met a car coming the other way. There was room to pass but Johnny forced the oncoming car to slow down, stuck his head out the window and shouted, 'Pig!' The other driver drove off, looked in his rear-view mirror and swore at Johnny … then his car hit the pig.

Maria and I had a lot in common musically. The Four
Seasons' 'December 1963 (Oh, What a Night)', Diana Ross
and 'Love Hangover', not forgetting Andrea True
Connection and 'More, More, More', and the still-popular
Hot Chocolate with 'You Sexy Thing'. We also loved
Queen's 'Bohemian Rhapsody' and the Eagles' 'Take it to
the Limit', while Paul McCartney had his 'Silly Love Songs'
– a little bit of everything. Because we had the car, we took
to going out to Blinkers nightclub at Leopardstown race-
course, racy pair that we were! We also took to making our
own cassette recordings of our favourite songs to play in
the car. Some of those cassette tapes exist to this day,
recorded on fine Sony Dolby tape, or, indeed, BASF. All was
fine, except when the tape would decide to get chewed in
the cassette player and we'd spend ages trying to fix it. We
couldn't even fling it out of the window in frustration,
because the tape had gone into the works of the player. Life
was so difficult in the seventies. And nowadays, people
don't understand the relationship between the cassette tape
and the pencil: if you had the former, you needed the latter.

These day trips were lovely, and a chance to get to know
each other and spend a day away, if possible. In truth, on
the southside we went as far as Greystones, and in north
Co. Dublin, to Skerries, but it took us quite a while to
muster up the courage to ask Maria's parents' permission
for us to go on our first foreign holiday. Sunshine, sangria,
sand, sea ... I'm missing something, but it'll come back to
me. We decided on the Canary Islands, an idyll for so
many Irish people, because they were close and warm, and

off we went to Playa del Ingles, on the south of Gran Canaria. On the flight over, we met two of my old school pals, Peter and Robert, who were staying in a lovely place, and we were staying ... some place else entirely. We'd elected to stay in an apartment block that had its own swimming pool, restaurant, money exchange and which was handy for the beach ... but, joy of joys, the late-night bar was directly under our apartment. Handy for the drink on the basis that you wouldn't get much sleep. We absolutely loathed it, but we were young and in love and, anyway, we'd be out all day, so we could handle it.

Well, we *were* out all day and we still hated the place. As you can see from the front cover of this book, I have the kind of complexion that would respond well to sunshine – it would beam down on me and I'd toast beautifully. Not so: within a couple of days, I began to resemble a plucked chicken. Now, it seemed to me that I was becoming acclimatised to the sun ... wrong. One evening, when we came back to our room, I could feel that my leg was particularly warm, slightly bumpy, in fact, too hot to touch. To my shrieks of appreciation, my lifelong companion applied a soothing balm and I left the leg hanging outside the bed for a bit of comfort, vowing not to turn on my side as I slept. The night passed, the morning came and it was time to look at the leg. Well, *dios mio*, as they say in Spain (I said something a lot worse): can you imagine what it would be like to wake up in the morning and find seven jellyfish had decided to make a home on your leg. Well, that's the sight that met us; the whole leg had ballooned in a succession of blisters.

Actually, I remember relating the story to a nurse friend of mine years later and she told me about a patient who had fallen asleep on the beach and got sunburned, ending up in hospital, where the doctor prescribed continuous intravenous feeding, a sedative and Viagra every four hours. My friend was astonished and asked the doctor, 'What good will the Viagra do him?' The doctor replied, 'It'll keep the sheets off his legs'. So the sunburn put paid to any thoughts I'd harboured of a sporty holiday on the old water skis, and Maria fell foul of the old Spanish tummy so, all in all, a jolly time was had by all.

Funny thing is, we kept in touch with the lads, Peter and Robert, and it was at Peter's family company, HB Dennis Motors, that I bought the car of my dreams. In school, I had always dreamed of getting an MGB Roadster. Of course, there was no chance of this happening as they were far too expensive and we were saving for the small matter of a wedding day (don't panic: there was no offer or acceptance at this point; just an understanding, but we were putting the money away as best we could). At this point, MG decided to stop making the Roadsters and HB Dennis had one left in the garage. Maria and I fell in love with it, in spite of the fact that it was yellow (it was the only one left, for heaven's sake).

What were the poor boy and girl to do? If we wanted to fulfil our dream, it would mean getting a loan and putting our big day on the long finger, but we both felt that if we let the moment pass, it would be gone for ever. So we bought the MGB for an astronomical sum, it seems to me now: £7,500. I have to say, we loved the car and it looked absolutely gorgeous, but had we known it would spend so much of its life in the garage being fixed, it might have lost some of its lustre that day. But it's wonderful to remember just how at one we were about that decision – we were clearly singing from the same hymn sheet.*

That MG brought me all over Ireland, quite often against its will, when I was touring the country as a Radio 2 DJ (of which more shortly). We are talking about an era when the roads were not so fab; there were no motorways, and back roads could stretch for 40 miles at a time, not to mention the potholes. The MG would be fine for a while, then on the way to Mullingar or somewhere, it would just pack in or start to get a bit sluggish and I'd have to pull into a local town to allow it to rest … and then it wouldn't start again. There were no mobile phones, so I became familiar with Garda stations, who would always help, letting me use the phone to call the venue and organising somebody to come and fix the car. (Another reason why rural Garda stations shouldn't be closed – they are too important.) Still, I could always settle back in the car while waiting for the tow truck, one of my cassettes playing one of the top bands of the day, and have an old rest.

* Here's a joke from a listener: a man is taking his son to school and he realises he's made an illegal turn at the lights. 'Oh, no, I just made an illegal turn,' says Dad. 'Don't worry,' says son, 'the police car behind us did the same thing.'

Actually, I remember one night, on a long drive from the west of Ireland home, I pulled into a garage forecourt in Portlaoise and proceeded to eat a sandwich and drink a cup of tea. After about ten minutes, there was a tap on my window (funny place for a tap, but I digress) and a Garda and a member of Ireland's Armed Forces were staring in at me. What was I doing? they asked me. I think they thought I was going to spring someone out of prison. I explained that I was having my sandwich and off they went, seemingly satisfied. In hindsight, had I explained the motoring history of the car, they would have understood that even if I had broken somebody out, they wouldn't get far!

...

It was certainly not a whirlwind courtship. Maria and I courted for ten years – we went and did our own things, as we'd just started out in life with new jobs and we wanted to experience it all before settling down, which we did after I wore Maria down after a number of marriage proposals. Third time lucky ... we got engaged in February 1985 and married six months later, in August. Once we'd made up our minds, there was no stopping us.

EARNING A LIVING

'Something in the Air'

Thunderclap Newman

Now, you might remember me telling you about my persistent efforts to get into national radio, having caught the bug on various independents. Well, in 1979, RTÉ came calling in the shape of Radio 2, or 2fm, and our lives changed completely. I left a blameless life in insurance on a salary that would sustain but hardly excite, to a salary that caused my father to almost drop his tea. The difference was immense, but so was the risk. I still to this day find it hard to imagine that at 23 years of age I was allowed on the national airwaves. (In some quarters they have been asking the same question ever since: how was this man allowed on the national airwaves?) But do it they did and so began a whole new life for me.

In retrospect, it might seem that this was always what I was going to do and yet it might never have happened. I have my bosses at PMPA, Enda Giles and, later, Tom Coughlan, to thank for those half-hour lunches that they approved, giving me the opportunity to do drivetime from Big D around the corner. Now that I think about it, perhaps it was a ploy to get me out of the company … only joking. About two thousand people applied for the jobs at the brand new station, and in the end only half a dozen of us ended up at RTÉ. These were heady days and the beginning of a whole new world of radio in Ireland. Almost immediately we became household names, joining the ranks of those already in RTÉ, like Larry Gogan, Vincent Hanley, Mark Cagney, Pat Kenny, Jimmy Greely and Ken Stewart. Along with me came Declan Meehan, Robbie Irwin, Gerry Ryan, Jim O'Neill, Ronan Collins and Dave Fanning.

My first show was broadcast live from Limerick and we went on air on 1 June 1979, six days before my 23rd birthday, so I was actually 22 … Janey mac! My first record was my favourite, 'Something in the Air' – as the years have passed, I've tended to start any new slot with that song. Maybe it brings good luck.

National radio was a whole new world to me. I'd really only dipped my toe in with pirate radio. The fear that came with this journey into the unknown was one thing, but the excitement of the road ahead gave every day such a buzz. Now, to say that every day was fantastic and all was well on a constant basis would be a lie. We were the new kids on the block and had to learn the ropes as we went, and there were those at the station who didn't see any point to our existence in the first place. Those who felt that the whippersnapper element had arrived and wondered what we could possibly add to their world. But of course it wasn't about their world: we were about creating our own parallel universe in the same building. At this remove, I suppose I can see where they were coming from, but when you're in your early twenties, as I was, you can be in quite a hurry; I wanted to fulfil my dream, because I'd been given the opportunity. With Billy Wall at the helm as station head, off we went.

I remember after a little while we started being asked to DJ around the country in nightclubs and village halls. It was great fun, and by all accounts our sets became quite the highlight in a local town – remember, there was no local radio at the time, Radio 2 or 2fm was it. When the DJ arrived in town, the hang sangwiches would be had with the committee and by 11.15, there might be 25 people in the hall; by midnight, the hall or nightclub would be hoppin', and once you'd be on, the floor would be full. You'd have competitions for T-shirts, mugs, records, in fact anything with the 2fm logo on it would be grabbed with open arms. I remember I'd play for an hour and a half and then head home. I drove myself, enjoying the spin (when the MG didn't break down, if you'll recall), but sometimes it could be a round trip of 10 hours. I'd get home and Mam would be up to see how it went and to make me a cup of tea. Some mammy.

The DJ thing lasted a few years at this level and then fizzled out. I actually remember doing a disco once in the middle of a field in Kilkenny and the star attractions, wait for it, were me and Richard Crowley, news broadcaster extraordinaire. I'm not sure if he read the news between tunes, but we got away with it. I would come home with a pocket full of bits of paper with requests for the radio show the following week, so it worked as a promotion as well as everything else.

I can still remember my first gig at the Greville Arms Hotel in Mullingar. The late gentleman Tommy Hayden was my agent, and he'd got me the gig, but I was a nervous wreck and really unsure of what to do in a country hotel context. When I had been with the pirate radio stations, I had played in Sloopy's disco in Fleet Street, and Hoops night-club, in which I worked along with two DJs from my pirate days, John Paul and Gerry Campbell. The man who ran Hoops, Larry Murrin, is now CEO of Dawn Foods and, as I write, President of IBEC. Should have stuck with him ... maybe.

I also DJ-d at Sardi's in the old South County Hotel, run by Krish Naidoo, a big noise in nightclubs at the time, and a gent. At Christmas I'd get a turkey as a gift – the only bird I ever pulled out there, as I used to joke. The mad thing about Sardi's was that I had to work in a spaceship affair suspended from the ceiling in the centre of the dance floor! I'd arrive with my music, collect a bucket and climb a rope ladder to my lofty perch, pulling the rope ladder up behind me. There I would remain for the best part of four hours. 'But hang on,' I hear you cry: 'What was the bucket for?' Let's just say, as the revellers below were dancing to 'The Rivers of Babylon', I was desperately holding on to mine, while eyeing the bucket! Show business, eh?

Thanks to my association with Krish and Tommy Hayden I ended up hosting Miss Ireland for some years, hence the appearance of Miss World at our wedding. Everything is connected really. There was also the Miss Hawaiian Tropic contest, which I hosted: sure you wouldn't know where to look. Anyway the point is, I wasn't exactly green in the nightclub DJ department.

But in Mullingar I was a mess with the nerves. In Ireland the so-called 'celeb' DJ was a new phenomenon and I didn't know what they expected or, indeed, what I expected of myself. Anyway, I went on, played the hits, played some games and dished out the giveaways and was in my car two hours later. All in all, a decent start, and so it went for the few years it lasted.

Meantime, back on the wireless, it was just an amazing time to work on radio in Ireland. We were at the beginning of legitimate pop music radio and, having been pirates, we got to see it from both sides. It was very different from pirate radio, because within RTÉ there are structures that have to be adhered to, rules of fairness and the like that certainly don't apply when you're a pirate, but putting the shows together, being on the committee that decided the radio playlist for the week and generally feeling a part of such an enterprise was very exciting. And to be given the chance to play the music I loved, getting to interview visiting stars like Meatloaf (more than slightly bananas), George Benson (sweetheart), Davy Jones ... in fact, I've a photograph of me with Davy Jones posing beside a bust of Seán Ó Riada in Radio Centre. It really doesn't get better than that, and on top of that, I had the opportunity to move into television. But radio was the thing for me – I was a music fan, first and foremost.

Until the arrival of 2fm, you listened to pirate radio here, you listened to BBC radio and Radio Luxembourg there, and there were the few hours a week that RTÉ radio gave over to music, with Larry Gogan or Ken Stewart, and that was it. So when RTÉ Radio 2 arrived, with the catchy slogan 'Cominatcha', it was quite a phenomenon and we were treated like celebrities. In your early twenties, this is not always the wisest of situations to find oneself in, but you make do. I found that I was being contacted by newspapers to see if I had an opinion about the latest car type, or fashion tips; I was asked for my thoughts on everything from the price of a loaf to my favourite style of jumper. Sometimes I'd ask myself, how did this suddenly happen? But it did, and quickly. I found myself in a brave new world full of excitement and adventure. It was exactly where I wanted to be and had done for years.

What was particularly good was that quite a few of us were new to this game so we all learned together and, I suppose, grew up together. I started out on the drivetime show, *Whelan Home*. My producer from the off was Robbie Irwin and we were together workwise for years. I trusted him and he trusted me, our friendship blossomed and we remain friends to this day. It was he I chose to be my best man when I married Maria, if you'll remember … no greater honour. For someone like me to find myself in the company of a master like Larry Gogan or, indeed, to have a nodding acquaintance with Mike Murphy, was quite the thrill. In any business, no matter what it is, when you arrive in, fresh-faced and eager, you're in a hurry and want to change the world, but you must respect those already there and particularly those who have been there a while – because they have shown their greatness over many years. When I think of the long careers of Larry, Gay Byrne, Brendan Balfe *et al*, or, in the UK, Terry Wogan, Jimmy Young, or Ken Bruce, I feel a sense of awe. Finding myself in the illustrious company of Irish greats made every day at 2fm seem special. Also, forging new friendships outside the radio building was very special.

One of my most treasured memories of this period is the friendship of Vincent Hanley. He was an absolute, fully fledged, top-of-the-bill and without-parallel star. 'Fab Vinnie' as he used to be called, was just that. When he came into a room he lit it up and he was constantly pushing the boundaries. He was also a wonderful companion, someone who shared my sense of humour and, just like Larry, he was a great source of inspiration and help to a newbie. Not only did we share the radio, but he invited me to be a part of *MTUSA* as a video jock, no less. Hence our friendship with Bill Hughes, who worked with Vincent on the television side of things.

Vincent was a colleague but he was also a friend, whose illness and subsequent death, so young, was such a shock to everybody. He was a bright light who died too soon and would have had, I have no doubt, an extraordinary life. He died in April 1987 at 33 years of age, and to this day, I keep his memorial card in the top drawer of my desk, so I can still summon him up in my mind when required.

His parents were lovely people, too, and I recall that, when he died, they offered me a memento of his answering machine – very cool at the time. Thrilled, I duly collected it and took it home to show Maria. (She gets to see all the good stuff.) Well, I couldn't wait to plug it in and show her how it worked – after all, this was quite an exotic addition to our house, quite apart from the fact that it had been Vincent's, so I plugged it in and … it exploded! Blooming thing was American! The hint was in the title of his television programme; *MTUSA*, and he'd been living in New York for some time. That was the end of my memento. In 2014, I was invited to unveil a plaque in his memory at his house in Kickham Street, Clonmel, Co. Tipperary, where Vincent's brother still lives. This coincided with what would have been Vincent's 60th birthday. It was a privilege to be part of such a special day.

...

Being in 2fm gave us access to a whole new world. For a record fan like myself, it was heaven. Records that I would normally have had to go into Dublin city to buy were being brought out to us free of charge; you'd want to see the state of the place on delivery day. Warner Music, Sony, EMI, RCA, Virgin, A&M, Arista, CBS; all these record labels and more would send a parcel of LPs and singles to each DJ/producer on a weekly basis. I was like a chocoholic who had broken into Cadbury's. You may recall, if you're paying attention, that I have always been a fan, of an act, of a singer, of a movie ... whatever. So, to find myself in this world, surrounded by all the goodies I had only dreamt of up to now was wonderful.

I remember my great friend Chris Roche, sadly also now gone, when he worked as a PR man for Warner Brothers. At the time, there was great excitement over Christopher Cross, who had set the world alight with his 1979 album of the same name, with songs like 'Ride Like the Wind', 'Sailing' and 'Never Be the Same'. He was on a European promotional tour in 1980 and Chris Roche had him coming into Ireland. In an effort to get an interview, we had to go in on Saturday and do a prerecord, which we duly did. Robbie Irwin came along and I brought Maria with me, and Chris, being a great PR man, had a cameraman with him. Interview done, album signed, pictures taken and off we went, delighted. The picture appeared in the paper a few days later with the caption, 'Pretty Dubliner Maria Dent meets her hero Christopher Cross'. Incidentally, she was sitting on his knee at the time. I've never been able to listen to 'Ride Like the Wind' in quite the same way since.

Chris Roche went on to be a big part of our lives as our friendship blossomed; he eventually moved out of the record industry, working for Jim Aiken, the great concert promoter. Chris became this larger-than-life figure loved by everyone in the industry. He would always be there for you for chats and laughs and he was a great brotherly figure to me, particularly when things wouldn't be going as well as I'd like. We would go for lunch, and that would last about five hours and we'd put the world to rights. He was so good for me and to me. He went much too young. This giant of a man was taken from us at the age of 44. I will never forget Christy Moore playing 'Ride On' at the funeral Mass, so poignant. Chris, for many reasons, was definitely the brother I never had, a wonderful, wonderful man. He was cool, funny, handsome and cynical, a big man in stature and big in heart, too.

Another friend who came my way out of the music industry and the wireless is Rory Golden (now a diving instructor), who thankfully is still with us and I owe him lunch. We became fast friends early on as well and I ended up as best man when he married the lovely Ann. Even though, on our drive to the church, I suddenly realised I had left the rings back at the house and we had to go back for them, he still remains my friend. God bless his patience. We share a love of life, of Spike Milligan jokes and of always looking on the bright side of life. That's the song that will take him out, but I hope it's not for a long, long time.

We had many mad occasions together but one in particular stands out, when Rory was working for Arista records and the great Barry Manilow came to Ireland to play the RDS. Rory, as only he could, got me an interview with Manilow, quite an achievement considering that on my radio shows, I had continually taken the mick out of the great crooner. I was the least likely person to get an interview with him and yet I really wanted one, and Rory obliged. The interview was arranged for before the concert (most unusual) and there I was with Rory, a mutual friend and record company executive from England, Maurice Goodwin, and the bould Barry. I don't know who was more nervous, Barry or me ... me, because I had my little tape recorder and I wanted to make sure it worked, and Barry, because as our time together wore on, the crowd outside seemed to get more and more boisterous and he seemed to get more and more concerned. Now, it seems to me that if you're a star at the peak of your powers, then you are likely to cause excitement among your people, but still, he seemed concerned for his own safety. But all went well and he went out to wow them and you know what, he wasn't half bad.

I suppose of all the shows I did, breakfast was the one I enjoyed most. I was in first, and I started the day off for myself as well as for everybody else. Getting the papers on the way in, coffee in hand and away we go. There was even smoking in the studio back then. Interacting with the listeners was a different matter in those days, before the advent of the internet. We didn't have that instant ability to look up anything or find out anything at a moment's notice; back then, if we didn't know the answer to a question, we had to check it out with a library or something. Books held the answers, not your phone or computer. No WhatsApp, no Twitter, no Facebook, no Google. When I was on the air and I got a response from the listener it was by phone, and for that I needed someone to be there to answer the phone. The producer coordinated the whole event and post was plentiful, often coming in with a response to something I might have said two days previously. Sounds crazy now, but that was how it was.

In the early eighties, we did the first 'Breakfast in America' broadcast with the station and it was such a buzz. The idea had been mooted for some time, but Kellogg's came on board as sponsor and made it a reality. What a great thing it was for a fellow from Killester to broadcast from New York City on the radio. I was like a mad thing. I had two producers, good heavens! My faithful friend Robbie and Jim Lockhart (a Horslip of note). A half dozen of us headed off and my friend Philip Nolan, now of the *Daily Mail,* then of the *Evening Herald,* and a great talent in the world of journalism, came along to report on our doings, for PR purposes, you understand. As the phrase goes, 'Hard times, Gay, but happy times'! To be honest, most of my time at the station was happy – how could it not be? This was the most fun you could possibly have while getting paid for it. Nothing could beat doing what I loved, surrounded by music and like-minded people, who only wanted to do the best we could. Life was good. Not every day was, but most were.

A pop quiz called *Thirty Years a Poppin'* marked my first foray into television. It began in 1982, 30 years since the charts had begun, funnily enough. No flies on us. When I look at stills from the show now, I look like a cross between Che Guevara and a Spanish waiter, with a moustache that could kill you at 50 paces. Nonetheless, this seemed to work well and was closely followed by the series *Video File*, a simple format in which stars came to Ireland, we interviewed them, added three or four videos and, hey presto, we had a programme. Working with great producer/directors like Ian McGarry and Bil Keating made my TV work such a pleasure and the learning curve was always a joy. Then there was the opportunity to become the first male presenter of a fashion programme called *head2toe*, with Frances Duff and my friend of 30 years, Mary O'Sullivan. So, all in all, as an old friend of mine would say, motoring well.

However! As in so many things there comes a time when you don't feel happy in yourself. By the mid-eighties, I had presented *Whelan Home*, the afternoon show and the breakfast show, when it was decided that I would return to a show called *Marty 'til Midnight*, which went out from 10 p.m. until, well, midnight, Monday to Friday. I'd presented the show for about a year in the early days, as it happened.

The boss at the time, Cathal McCabe, felt that my appeal to a young audience, particularly students, would help the station at night-time. Now, you can take this any way you want but I took it as a demotion and felt aggrieved. I knew from previous experience, having hosted the show, that I had a link with that audience and could certainly pull in the numbers. I knew their music, I knew what they were into and I was always very particular about responding to them on the programme and building up a very strong following. And yet, and yet. I didn't really want to go back to night-time, because I'd been there, done that. There was also the small matter of my having gotten married in 1985 and, quite honestly, I didn't feel like being out of the house five nights a week. I was beginning to get itchy feet.

Meantime, back on television, I got my very own quiz show on Sunday evenings called *Where in the World?*, developed by the aforementioned great Bil Keating and techno wiz Danny McNally. Bil also produced the show, in which two families of four battled it out for a big holiday prize. So I started this show as a big autumn player on RTÉ 1 television in 1987 and presented it for two seasons. Working with Bil was brilliant, because not only was he, and is he, very talented, but he's a wonderful man to be around, a kind and decent soul.

Just to add to this workload, Maxi and I found ourselves co-hosting the National Song Contest in 1987 at the Gaiety Theatre, and from there I was asked by Ian McGarry to compère the Eurovision Song Contest that year. This was at the Palais du Centenaire in Brussels and guess who our representative was, only Johnny Logan with 'Hold Me Now'. So, the very first Eurovision Song Contest I get to attend as commentator and we win it – what are the chances? Johnny sang his heart out in his lovely white suit and melted the hearts of Europe. See, good song, good singer equals great result. But I meander as I'm prone to do. More of Eurovision later; it deserves a section all to itself. (Yes, says you, and preferably behind a high wall!)

As I write this, my leaving RTÉ doesn't strike me as a particularly good move, nor might it give the reader much faith in my judgement, but this is now and I'm writing about how I felt at the time. In television, I was flying and who knew what might come next, but in radio, I felt I was stagnating, going nowhere; if anything, going backwards. I couldn't understand how, with such a high-profile television career, I found myself on radio in the middle of the night. I felt that one should complement the other: if you have somebody with a high profile who is doing well in one medium, then you capitalise on it in the other. But that wasn't happening. After all, the radio career was five days a week and I needed to feel confident and secure in it and in no way to feel that I could be dispensed with.

In 1988, a producer called Louis Hogan, with whom I'd always got on very well, left the station to run a temporary radio station, Millennium 88 FM, out of the GPO in Dublin for the city's millennium celebrations. Those who joined him on this temporary expedition included Gareth

O'Callaghan, Jimmy Greeley, Robbie Irwin, Declan Meehan, Scott Williams, Maxi and others. With the departure of these people quite a number of allies had left the building. I was invited to join them and think about it I did, but I didn't really want to go. However, something was at me to do something: I just didn't feel the love where I was.

By this stage, the late eighties, the idea had begun to take shape of having a national independent radio station. A man called Oliver Barry, who was a businessman and promoter, had mooted the idea, and others like Terry Wogan and Chris de Burgh had added their names as directors. There was even talk of a national independent TV station. A whole new world was opening up and it was easy to be enticed into it, particularly as I had itchy feet at 2fm.

Now you're probably thinking, this eejit needed some help of the therapy kind. The fact is, I talked about a move elsewhere with Maria, with my folks and with those people I felt closest to, and there's no doubt when you're feeling a little vulnerable and somewhat at sea, you can get despondent and I felt that at the time. In hindsight I was actually operating from a position of strength, but felt that I wasn't. And therein lies the rub in this business – even when things appear to be as good as they can be, they may not be.

All my working life had been heading towards this place, this position where I found myself on national radio five days a week, happy as a pig in the proverbial, so the idea of walking out the gate and not returning was completely and utterly against everything I stood for and, quite frankly, frightened the life out of me. Having spent all those years working towards doing what I wanted to do every day with like-minded people, leaving just didn't sit right with me. On the other hand, rarely are you in control of events in this business, so to have some degree of control over my own destiny would be tempting. To be actively sought by another radio station, with everything that came with that, promised that sense of control.

The easiest thing in the world was to do nothing, so I found myself sitting on the fence and letting things progress as they would. Of course, there were conversations about joining this national independent radio station, but they were just conversations. Being frustrated in your job is one thing, but to walk away from it on the basis that there will be no frustration elsewhere, while doing the same job, is naïve. Perhaps I was naïve, but that's easy to say from here. The rumour circling at the station was that changes were afoot, but at the same time, if you were seen talking to anybody, rival radio stations, for example, all hell would break loose and you could find yourself on the outside anyway. Another concern for me was the possibility that I could lose all my TV work if I left. It hadn't been done much before. At that time in RTÉ, if people left, they left. Off to see what the world would bring them and to try their hand at something elsewhere. Some would keep an element of their RTÉ business alive and so it all seemed amiable and quite doable. The problem for me was, who, professionally, would I ask if a move would work for me? Remember, back in the late eighties, there were no other radio stations, there was no other TV channel: it was quite the leap of faith. I suppose had I been heading off to the UK, as others had before me, it wouldn't have made much difference because I'd be over there, everyone else would be here and never the twain would meet. What if I only moved a tiny bit along the dial on the wireless? The 'wireless knob', as Paul Durcan would say. The what ifs and the what if nots circled in my head; a great sheaf of papers with the pros on one side and the cons on the other was filled. Would I stay put, or take a leap into the unknown? Quite often you have to embrace that fear and go with it, but I wasn't brave, or so I thought. What is the great line: 'Better be a coward for a day than a dead man all your life'? If you never stick your head above the parapet, then the chances of anybody lopping it off are fairly slim. I hadn't, thank God, had to deal much with failure during my tenure and quite honestly didn't imagine I'd have to deal with it much in the future. I had a lot of soul-searching to do.

I have to laugh rereading some of this because while all this cacophony was going on in my head, I hadn't been offered anything and yet somehow knew it was coming. The phrase I definitely kept close to my heart around this time was a great one of Spike Milligan's: 'Behind every silver lining there's a cloud.'

...

And so began the dance of the Century.

'Cycles'

Frank Sinatra/Gayle Caldwell

Well, the approaches and then the calls came, from a new independent radio station, Century Radio. As the idea of this independent radio station took shape, all manner of names were bandied about, meetings were held in hotels and offices across the city and, sure enough, I got the call. It was somebody else's dream and I was to be a part of it. With Oliver Barry at the helm (a former senator, member of the RTÉ authority, a promoter who had brought such names as Michael Jackson and Prince to Ireland and who was hugely respected), and a board that included my hero Terry Wogan, the prospect was certainly eye-catching. One of the most impressive men in the radio industry, Mark Storey, was going to be head of programmes – if ever there was a reason to join another radio station it was because he was there. We had known and liked each other from his time at 2fm (he came with huge experience from the UK and has subsequently soared to heady heights in commercial radio over there). Another bright spark was Keith Pringle, who eventually ended up as managing director of the UK's biggest commercial station, Capital Radio in London. Add to this exciting new state-of-the-art equipment and studios and being sold a vision of a brave new world in radio ... well, we all wanted to believe it. As I had been a huge fan of Terry Wogan all my life, the idea of being a part of the station of which he was a director and presenter was very exciting. It seemed that a whole new world was opening up for me, if I signed to Century: a new TV channel for Ireland was on the horizon, plus there was the possibility of TV and radio work in the UK. But first, it required my leaving RTÉ radio and possibly losing my work in television. There was a lot at stake.

To say the prospect made me sick to my stomach is to understate it, yet I felt a need to grasp this opportunity with both hands. I was totally and utterly terrified of the idea and yet strangely drawn, like a moth to a light.

I made the move late one evening in a solicitor's office in town, having had the 'welcome aboard' phone call from Terry before I'd signed on. Sure I was a goner with the phone call, wasn't I? Louis Hogan, who acted for me, and who was someone I had greatly admired in 2fm, felt confident about the move, as did I. In retrospect, weren't we the bright fellas? It was only having signed with Century that I got the nod the breakfast show was mine once again on 2fm, but it was too late. I was off.

For as long as I live, I don't think I will ever forget that evening and the fear, mixed with excitement, that gripped me. There were no mobile phones at the time so, once I'd signed on the dotted line, I pulled in to a phone box and rang Maria. I explained that I had signed (obviously she knew in advance) but I needed to hear her reassuring voice. This I did, but with her customary caution. How right she was, too.

Heading off into the unknown was a daunting prospect but the entire proposal seemed like such an adventure that you just wanted to be on board for it. See, there's that lad taking the chance again. I had never seen myself as a risk-taker, but I was wrong. It's hard to explain now, but there was such an air of optimism about the launch of Century and all things seemed possible. What could go wrong?

...

Century Radio opened on 4 September 1989 on 100–102 FM to great razzmatazz. There was a party atmosphere on the day at the station's headquarters up in Christchurch, in the heart of Dublin. There was a general air of goodwill towards the station and the fact that something brand new was happening in radio. How brand new, in retrospect, was arguable, but the fact remains, this was the first national independent radio station in Ireland and, as such, deserves some plaudits.

I wasn't the only one on board from the actual national station, by the way, oh no: Robbie Irwin, Richard Crowley, Jimmy Greely, David Harvey, John Saunders, Catherine Maher, Declan Meehan, all were there, as well as sports and news journalists, including David Davin Power. Added to this there was the *Terry Wogan Show* on Saturdays and really good sports coverage. Even the jingles were state of the art, all the way from JAM Creative Productions in Dallas.

I loved being with people I liked and listening to the late Bob Gallico chatting with Declan and the warmth of Jimmy's voice in the morning. Liam Quigley and Owen Larkin's, too. The great producer and later author Pat Dunne joined us, too, as did Paddy Clancy and Emer Woodfull, and who could forget the shy and retiring Claire McKeown. I give you this list to illustrate the quality of the people behind and in front of the microphone. This was no cobbled-together bits-and-bobs enterprise, but, in fact, a very credible, decent radio station.

We had what was quite the thing at the time, 'zoo radio', which relied on the back-and-forth between a team, rather than on a single voice. I was presenter and around me were Dave Harvey doing news, John Saunders (now of Fleishman Hillard) on sport, and Catherine Maher on anything that took her fancy. We had great fun and it was all a bit madcap. I also took on a Saturday show and really enjoyed it. We'd have a guest in and have the chat, which I always love. As an interviewer, you have an idea of how you want the interview to go and the topics you want to touch on, but I love how a conversation can just drive the interview along and make it more real. It's a conversation first and foremost, now let's see where it goes. The great and the good came to see us: Mary Robinson, Paddy Maloney, Gilbert O'Sullivan, Garrett Fitzgerald, Bob Geldof *et al*. One of my favourite memories is of Paul Brady sitting in front of me, playing his guitar and singing 'Arthur McBride' and 'The Lakes of Pontchartrain'. These are the privileges that come with this business.

Because of the station's links with Capital Radio in London I also got to interview a couple of beauties over there. As part of a fact-finding expedition, seeing how things were done over the water, I popped into Chris Tarrant's breakfast show along the way in Capital (he had millions of London listeners every day and this was before the heady heights of *Who Wants to Be a Millionaire?*). Because of the Capital connection, for our show I got to interview Richard Branson and Kenny Everett. This was a whole new world opening up in front of me. I recall a train journey with a senior executive from Capital Radio as we enjoyed a gin and tonic and talked of future plans – for a fella who had dreamed of being on radio years ago, this was exciting stuff.

...

Those involved worked so hard to make Century succeed, but it seemed as if the gods were against us from the outset. The problems started early on, when some people got in touch with the station to say they couldn't hear it. Now, that's loyalty at an alarming level. Coverage was intermittent across the country. Apparently you could be driving down a country road listening away, you'd turn left behind a mountain and we'd disappear ... now, that's magic! It was clear that the coverage wasn't as national as we'd have hoped. Added to that, the station apparently lost a packet on advertising that never quite materialised and, all in all, it became a bit of a wear-out from day to day. I felt that things were not going well near the end of our second year of transmission when the plants in the foyer disappeared. That was one thing, but when the toilet paper starts disappearing from the loo, you know it's time to start packing! But the station battled on ... I suppose lurched is a better word (also referred to in Cork as a clinger!).

We could feel it on a day-to-day basis. The transmission had in fact improved greatly by the second year and we were getting listeners, but the damage had been done, and, even though management came and went like managers in the Premier League, we all had to believe that the station would one day work itself into a position of strength. I recall when a man with plastic shoes and a title I didn't quite get arrived from the UK and told us he'd all the answers. We went for lunch and he asked me to tell him about my career to date and I think that was the moment when I realised this might not end well. Within weeks he was gone and someone else arrived with the same idea, only slightly different. These people are called radio doctors. Now, don't get me wrong, some of them are very able. It's just that when we had to deal with them, the able ones seemed to be elsewhere. I recall a conversation with one of them who told me that he had no particular interest in Ireland beyond Newlands Cross, it was about Dublin and outside just didn't exist. I had come from a national radio background and was fairly taken aback by the attitude.

At this stage, Capital Radio in London expressed an interest in buying the station and certainly could have from a financial point of view, but the rules of the time and the vagaries of a world unknown to us deemed it not possible. So, at 6 p.m. on a November evening in 1991, the station simply closed down. My colleague Claire McKeown was about to go on air and ... that's it, good luck now and ... silence.

It came as a huge shock, in spite of the rumours. I found myself on *RTÉ News* expressing dismay at the situation, and the following day the papers were out taking pictures and asking what my plans were. Like I had any. We needed to regroup as a family: the one thing that was truly wonderful about this period had been the arrival of Jessica in September 1990, but this meant that the Whelan family had gotten bigger and was more in need than ever before. Maria was still working in Aer Lingus at the time, but our world had shattered. The phone stopped ringing. I wasn't useful to people any more. I am reminded of the Monty Python sketch about being an 'ex-parrot'. I was now an 'ex-radio presenter' and it was a pretty empty feeling. It was also very scary. So, what to do now and how to do it?

There was an attempted revival of the station but it came to nothing, and I realised that I was out of a job. Alternative plans needed to be put in place. Guess what? Guardian angel time. Along came Jeannie and the rest of her merry gang from Saatchi & Saatchi and asked me if I'd like to front a campaign for Daz washing powder in Ireland. I hesitated for about five seconds. If you wanted to get your whites whiter, I was your man. Tell you one thing, it sustained us at a time when we didn't know which way to turn. Quite frankly, had it come to it, I would have eaten the stuff.

The amazing thing about doing that ad campaign on TV was that it meant I was still out and about meeting people and being back on television and, after a couple of years away at Century, viewers remembered me. But being remembered can bring its own trauma too. Before Daz arrived I had to deal with the reality of signing on the dole. This had never happened to me before and had I stayed in PMPA all those years ago, I might have avoided it. But it had to be done, because I had a family to support. I'll never forget the feeling inside when I approached the dole office in the centre of Dublin. I was scared, mortified, defeated, lost in a world I didn't understand. I can still see myself heading for the door and then walking past it and going around the block a second time, ringing home to tell Maria I couldn't do it, yet knowing I had to. Eventually I plucked up the courage from somewhere, went inside and signed on.

One of the more positive aspects of this period was the support I received from people on the street. Taxi men, particularly, would roll down their window and tell me, 'Miss you on the radio, you'll be okay, son', or, 'Don't worry. Chin up, you'll be back'. People were kind and it meant a huge amount. One of the things I've always believed is that a kind word can go a long way; it certainly did in my case.

I missed the radio but I had to get over that because our survival was what really counted here. I did notice over a fairly short period of time that a number of colleagues from Century were returning to RTÉ but in my case, after various attempts, the door was firmly shut. There were individuals who felt that I'd made my bed and I could lie in it. Funny, they didn't apply the same logic to others. I have heard stories about meetings at which my name was mentioned for consideration, and the immediate response was that I would not be welcome back at the station. I have to say that I don't bear any grudges. I'm not bitter about things in any way. I understand that I took a risk and it didn't work out, and I bear no ill will to anyone, but one thing I learned from my exile was that other people didn't feel the same way: maybe it doesn't matter any more, but it mattered then and it would be 12 years before I would return to radio.

Meanwhile, over to the telly! You see, I had lost my three TV shows when I left RTÉ (even though I really didn't think I would), so a return to television didn't seem all that easy. Surprisingly, the good folks at RTÉ television seemed to have no truck with the attitude prevailing in radio. Over a period of time, I met with various people and hoped against hope that somebody would make a move. Funnily enough, that move came with a telethon, in 1992 if memory serves, a show produced by Moya Doherty, whose partner, John McColgan, had been the main man when I presented my first TV show, the pop quiz. I found myself standing behind a door on the set holding a cheque that someone had donated. I knocked on the door, Ireland's legendary host, Gay Byrne, opened the door and said, 'Look who we have here', and I was back. From here began a series of conversations, particularly with Liam Miller, a man who could make things happen, and he did. He assured me that television had no axe to grind, no issue whatsoever and that as long as he had something for me to do, I could do it.

It's hard to explain what this felt like to Maria and myself. Even though we didn't have anything concrete, the relief was immense, because there was the small matter of having to continue to feed the child, which was uppermost in our minds. In any situation like this you require people who believe in you and can see what you bring to a project. Otherwise you get nowhere. I was very fortunate that a number of people were there for me when I needed them. I've mentioned the great Bil Keating of *Where in the World?* fame, with whom I'd worked on programmes like *John Player Tops of the Town* on TV for 10 years, and Ian

McGarry, both hugely talented men as producer/directors with a strong musical background.

Also, daytime television in RTÉ was in an expansionist mood with a man called Noel Smyth, who was very innovative and incredibly supportive of me, at the helm. He had successfully steered the legendary *Live at Three* for some years to great acclaim and he had a plan. Out of the blue he rang me one day, explained that he'd like to meet me for coffee and I think by the time he had boiled the kettle, I had made the journey from Portmarnock, where I lived, to Donnybrook. He felt that with all those radio days behind me, I might just be the man to take on a new role in daytime television, because I was 'not afraid to be live', as the saying goes. Well, we started with little beginnings, doing continuity between programmes here and there, adding a little bit along the way, an interview here and there, always building it up, until he created a new series, *12-2-1*, which I co-presented with Ciana Campbell. Meantime, back in the variety department, there was *Off the Record*, a chat show with guests and the RTÉ Concert Orchestra, which is where I got to meet greats like Spike Milligan and John Hume and so many more. We had two seasons of the series and even had 'Marty Parties' to launch them. Happy days. Then came the talent series *Go For It*, which was an RTÉ/BBC Northern Ireland co-production. Here, I was joined by David Blake Knox as head of department, Kevin Lenihan as producer and Bob Corkey as director. We had such a time of it for two seasons.

Which reminds me of a nice story. I recall working in Belfast during the period of the Apprentice Boys' march. The four of us were standing on the street and I felt particularly nervous, even though everyone else seemed relaxed. That black Northern Irish humour came to the fore when our BBC producer, the late Harry Adair, a lovely, talented man, came up close to my ear and went 'Bang!' They all fell about laughing while the lads in the sashes marched on.

Then, having worked with the National Lottery on a weekly draw from time to time in the Royal Hospital Kilmainham, they decided they'd like a summer show, and *Millionaire* was born. The concept was one show across the summer and a guarantee of £1 million for the winner. At the end of summer 1995, we handed over a cheque for £1 million. The success of *Millionaire* led to the great Ray Bates, then head of the National Lottery and RTÉ coming up with a summer show called *Fame and Fortune*, which I went on to present for 11 years. (Wait for it now, hang on, I have it: 'How do you play?' 'You buy a ticket.' Should have patented that years ago.)

It was a long way from the dole office. I thoroughly enjoyed the company of Ian, Bil, David, Noel and Kevin. It was fun, it was exciting and we were always creating something and it meant a lot that at that level, people saw that I had a value – it was very heartening. Then on daytime, I found myself in the company of Thelma Mansfield, Ciana Campbell, Mary Kennedy and Alf McCarthy on an afternoon show called *PM Live,* which ran for a couple of years, closely followed in 1999 by the arrival of (trumpet blast please) *Open House.* Add to this the Rose of Tralee Festival every August for six years, beginning in 1997, with Noel Smyth as executive producer and Dave Donaghy as director. That was fun. And it was fun to be busy on the telly.

Of all the shows we did, the one with the most contact with the public in a real sense was *Fame and Fortune* with the National Lottery. Every week we had our contestants, who were full of beans, and then an audience who would be high as kites, thanks to the RTÉ/Lottery kindness in hostility (hospitality without the smile) before the show. Up to their necks in canapés and Cabernet Sauvignon! The show was also great for the trips that were organised as part of the prize for the viewers at home. If you remember, it was an extra piece of business on the scratch card for viewers at home. You scratched off 'USA' for an American trip, 'Paris', 'Rome', and so on. Then, each week, a name was pulled out and you and a pal/partner were off to that destination with 80 or so other happy campers. There were those, I kid you not, who believed I flew out every week with a couple for a week's holiday! Sure I'd be worn out with all the flights. But the standard that the Lottery set itself was so good that no one could complain. Nothing was left to chance, apart from the winning of the prizes, which was pure chance. The lucky winners were so pleased that there was a carefree air for the entire trip, plus the fact, as the Lottery pointed out to me, they always gave them spending money. You can always win a holiday, but who knows your circumstances, so the easiest thing is to give you the wherewithal to enjoy yourself when you get where you're going. They've made dreams come true for so many.

Paris is always magical and we had a couple of great trips there. Dinner would be arranged for all the winners by the Lottery and it would always be in a good restaurant. I remember once we went to the Jules Verne restaurant in the Eiffel Tower, where a sumptuous meal was presented to us. All was well until it began to dawn on our winners that potatoes would not be forthcoming. An air of mutiny filled the Eiffel Tower, not for the first time, but calm was restored when eventually *pommes frites* arrived, *mon Dieu*!

We also had a wonderful trip to Rome, the Eternal City (apparently the people of Japan also refer to the city of Kyoto as the Eternal City; bet I know which one serves the best pizza though). While in Rome it was suggested that I would really enjoy a bike ride. Now, cycling in Rome is only for those who have a death wish, quite frankly, but I agreed to it. Not on the road – I'm not a complete eejit – but at the top of the Spanish Steps. You head towards the Pincian Hill and the Villa Borghese gardens. It's lovely and seems to go on for ever. When I got back, I limped through the foyer with the air of one who wouldn't last long enough to pay his bill.

Of all the cities I've visited in this lifetime (if I believed in reincarnation, I could have been somewhere else before, do you get me?), I love Rome the most. It's the incredible history on every street, the architecture, the food and wine, the beauty of the people, both men and women, and the fact that, in general, they couldn't be bothered with you … Actually quite refreshing. They drive like lunatics, roar at each other all the time and I just love it with a passion, sorry, *passione*.

We crossed the Atlantic to New York a number of times, once on Concorde, arriving shortly after we left Ireland! That was terrific and it's sadly gone now. We were due to fly on it again, shortly after it crashed in Paris. It was incredible to fly at twice the speed of sound, while quaffing champagne. We also crossed from Southampton to New York on *Queen Elizabeth 2* (please desist – the boat, not Her Majesty) and it was marvellous. To cap it all, the voyage was so bumpy that hundreds of people were seasick – we were sailing through the tail end of a hurricane. But calm was restored. Then there was a Caribbean cruise on the same ship another year calling at Grenada, St Kitts and St Thomas and the like … truly incredible and a prize to savour.

When you plan these trips in advance, as the Lottery obviously does, you have no idea what might occur between the planning date and that of the trip. In fact, it used to be a running joke that if you came on a trip with me and the Lottery, anything could happen. On our recent *Winning Streak* trip to San Francisco, I was chatting to our assembled winners and said, 'We'll have a great time, please

God, but I can't guarantee you an earthquake, even with my reputation.' Lo and behold, the following morning ... earthquake! It wasn't me, honest – actually, we slept through it. On a more sombre note, on one of our New York trips, we were due to take dinner in the Windows on the World restaurant at the top of the World Trade Center in September 2011, the week the towers fell.

All these trips have been put together by Denis, Barbara, Paula and Eddie and a host of other National Lottery luminaries, who have ensured that everyone had the best time possible. Because that's what the National Lottery does, makes dreams come true. I am eternally grateful to them for the travel stickers they've made it possible for me to put on my suitcase.

Trips aside, my relationship with the National Lottery stretches back the best part of 25 years – now, that's a strong relationship. Ray Bates, former director of the Lottery, always had a positive air about him and pushed for the Lottery to bring out the fun in itself, while always making sure the good causes were front and centre, a tradition that has continued with the current director, Dermot Griffin. Ray and his lovely wife Mary have been friends of ours for many years; she's a gifted artist and a lady. They are a couple of swells, whose friendship we cherish.

I've always felt that the decision I made in conjunction with Kevin Linehan and David Blake Knox in late spring or early summer 1995 to go for *Millionaire* was to change our lives in the best possible way. It led to an almost unbroken record of being on a National Lottery TV show every year since, it determined how each year would be structured from a family point of view and it gave me a very real link with the viewer at home, in the armchair, unable to move after a big dinner and a pint of milk and stuck with me for an hour or so. That link has proven to be so important, because, let's face it, if you make a TV show and nobody watches, then the TV show ain't coming back and neither are you. That's the joy of *Fame and Fortune* and *Winning Streak*; this is real people's television. We are a small island and the chances are that even if everybody doesn't know everybody, somebody knows somebody on the show, and that's part of the fun of it. There's also the thing where somebody clearly well off is on the show and you watch it in the hope that they don't win, or there's the person just out of work who really needs a few bob and you watch to the bitter end, willing them to win. I'm fully aware that there is an element out there who watch to see what people are wearing (the ladies anyway). And from working with Kathryn Thomas, Jeri Maye and Sinead Kennedy (as well as Mary Kennedy and Ciana Campbell in the past) I also know that what they get up to with wardrobe in RTÉ causes phones to ring on a Monday morning.

But the real joy of these National Lottery programmes is the Irish people. They are the real stars of the show. When contestants come into RTÉ for the show, they can either be incredibly nervous or incredibly cocky – it just depends, but the hair will definitely be done, the outfit bought and the teeth whitened … and that's just the men. As it's a game of chance, no one is ever going to be made to look foolish, because that just isn't how I operate. Before we make the show, we spend the day getting to know each other, chatting about this and that and rehearsing how all the games work, so that by the end of it all, we are ready to make it for real. The really important part of the job is to make sure that each player is as comfy as possible, because if it's rabbit-in-the-headlights time, then everybody at home will know. You can't hide the look of terror from the viewer. It's the telly, for God's sake, they see everything. But generally speaking, it always works out okay, and as for the winnings? You came in with a three-euro investment and no matter what happens, you've turned it into thousands of euro. Do you know any banks offering the same deal? Like I say; 'How do you play? You buy a ticket.' Is it too late to patent that now?

It has been noted that I seem to find myself with these marvellous female co-presenters on television, who eventually find themselves in the arms of others. Can't understand it. Someone said to me recently, 'Now that you're writing the book, you should list the female partners you've had on the telly.' Why this is deemed necessary, I'll never know, but here goes: Ciana Campbell, Thelma Mansfield, Mary Kennedy, Mary O'Sullivan, Frances Duff, Maxi, Kathryn Thomas, Jeri Maye, Sinead Kennedy – and six years of the Rose of Tralee times 32 roses comes out at 192! No wonder I'm worn out. The format of male/female presenter-led shows has always been a popular idea and generally works, although I do recall a number of occasions on UK television where the animosity between the two of them was evident, but thankfully I've never had any problems. It's all about generosity of spirit on both sides: you can get in each other's way if you're not careful, so the trick is not to. Be aware that the other person has valid things to say and points to make. I was going to tell you about the time … and, well … a gentleman never tells. What I can say is that having a partner on a TV show can be a very good thing because the banter and fun makes the viewer connect with us and vice versa. That was part of the charm of *Open House* – the rapport between myself and Mary and the fun we were having.

I'm often asked if I prefer radio or television. The simple answer is that both have their moments. Both are broadcasting to you but the radio is one-to-one. It keeps you company wherever you are and it really is more personal. You can be anywhere listening to the radio, including the bath or in your car or lounging in the garden or climbing a mountain or … heaven forbid. Whereas with TV the assumption is that you are in your living room after your tea and sitting comfortably, paying attention. But being on the telly means everybody knows you and that familiarity is actually a lovely thing to behold. In general, people mean well; there are very few people who actually want to hurt or upset you. I tend to keep out of pubs after 10 p.m., when lads tend to get a bit 'shouty'. I do recall the Mike Murphy story, where this fellow came up to him, obviously a lovely man, and said to Mike: 'I can't stand you, and the wife, she can't stand you. And she knows nothin'.' What a wonderful man he would be to spend time with.

The truth is, not everybody is going to like you, that's just not the way the world operates, so after you figure that out, some 20 years into your career, you begin to settle down and get on with it. As Gay Byrne said to me once, 'As long as more than 50 per cent like you, you'll be okay.' American presidential elections are won on that basis!

...

I called this chapter 'Cycles', because that's what this business is like; everything goes in cycles. Sometimes you're flavour of the month, sometimes not. Sometimes you'll make foolish decisions, sometimes good ones – who is it who said, there's no such thing as a 'good' decision, only a decision? When I joined RTÉ Radio 2 all those years ago, I had no idea where my career would take me – it's certainly had its ups and downs, but that's life. The whole thing reminds me of the song itself. 'Cycles' is Frank Sinatra's take on the Gayle Caldwell song about being down and out, trying to hide, but remembering that spring always comes. Something better always comes along in time. How true.

'Wichita Lineman'

Glen Campbell/Jimmy Webb

I have loved this song from the time I first heard it at my mother's knee. It just evokes an image of this lonely man up on a telegraph pole and all these conversations going on around him in the middle of Wichita, Kansas. Songwriter Jimmy Webb was able to conjure up an image that has stayed with us for many years. It is a song that remains in my top three of all time. And to have it played by the man himself on the telly, on the piano, actually – well, that was quite the moment. But then on *Open House*, the afternoon show I presented on television with Mary Kennedy for six years between 1999 and 2004, there were many such moments.

When you work on a programmme like *Open House* a whole new world opens up to you, and I was grateful for that, all the more so because of what had gone before, having survived the end of Century Radio. The new daytime show was commissioned to be made by Tyrone Productions, the people who brought you *Riverdance*. They knew what it was to have two fine people out front performing like mad things while a whole troupe worked behind them for the common good. And so it was on *Open House,* with a great team of researchers and producers and a plan to make exciting television in the afternoon. And you know what, I think we did, actually.

Doing a programme five days a week for an hour and a half a day requires steely determination and a real sense of what the viewer wants, merging entertainment with real-life stories in a programme that looks at what's going on around it, to reflect who we are. We covered the practical, be it gardening or art appreciation or cookery, but we also involved ourselves in the topics of the day, getting the viewer involved, too. It was an interactive programme before its time.

Well, Mary and I took to it like ducks to water.* And so off we went on our merry journey, and you know what? For most of the time it really was. We had the great Dermot

---

* You're thinking now it must be time for a joke involving a duck. If you think this is the sort of cheap read that would stoop to belittle a passing mallard, you'd be absolutely right. It's the one about two Belfast ducks who were strolling along the street when one says, 'Quack', and the other one says, 'I'm going as quack as I can'. I find on a daily basis that being subjected to this level of humour is actually good for you.

O'Neill in the garden, many fine contributors on a weekly basis, and we also met up with Neven Maguire of MacNean House and Restaurant in Blacklion, Co. Cavan. With Neven, the story goes that John Masterson, the executive producer and all-round good egg, was looking for a regular chef for the show. Reg Looby, a foodie and expert in the field, suggested Neven and said to the aforementioned JM that he just had to try this guy. Well, he did. Neven clicked with us and we with him and the rest is history. The restaurant, founded by his parents Joe and Vera Maguire back in 1989 and named after the MacNean Lakes, had been doing well, anyway. There were nine children in the Maguire family and all played a part, but it was Neven who fell in love with cooking, as he says himself, 'by walking round the kitchen at my mother's knee'. And boy, did he learn.

We met Neven in 1998; that's a long time ago and he didn't give the appearance of a fellow who had started to shave yet. He was, in fact, 25, and in 2003 he took over the business as head chef and proprietor. He would have achieved culinary greatness anyway, but there's no doubt that his time on *Open House* propelled him into the public consciousness, where he has remained, successful and much loved, ever since. And I have an expanding waistline to prove it. Funnily enough, Mary Kennedy never put on an ounce. I think she took the food home to her family! In fact, you can see from the photograph that we all had slimness on our side. (Speaking of food, a question: how do you stop sandwiches from curling? Answer: take away the brooms. Suit yourself.)

Actually it's amazing, when I think back now, how many people came through our famous portals: Aidan Power, who has gone on to great things, started with us as a boy reporter, and Mr Brendan Courtney, who started with us as a researcher and who could dress you at 50 paces and criticise what you were wearing at the same time. But you see, this was the secret of *Open House*. To work in an environment like *Open House* requires a real sense of camaraderie, of teamwork, of 'one for all and all for one', well, two, in this case, because it was Mary and me. Being the presenter places you centre stage, but you're only as good as the research that you were given and how the producer puts it together, how the director shoots it and, only then, how we present the piece. We were lucky to have Dolores Comerford as producer, and, among others, Justin McColgan as director; John Masterson and then Larry Masterson (no relation), who will soon take over the reins of the *Late Late*, were both executive producers on the show. In TV, particularly on a live show like this one, there are so many people involved before the show even starts. There's wardrobe and make-up, two of my favourite haunts. Make-up can cover up a multitude and make you look almost presentable, while wardrobe can do the same thing with a decent suit; sorted! Quite frankly, if it wasn't for Brigette Horan (who has dressed me from the RTÉ wardrobe since the beginning), I'd be lost. Brigette has seen me through flares, drainpipes, pinstripes, dress suits and the rest. Thank God we haven't got to the expanded waist – yet! But there's time. My current wife has the greatest taste. And between her and Brigette, I rarely leave home looking less than spic and span. But on the telly, I wouldn't look a stitch as stylish as I do, only for Brigette.

So now you look the part, but you still have to go into a studio and be ready for the red light. In the studio, there are sound people, cameras, a floor manager, stage manager, someone in your ear from the control box and a guest waiting for you whose name you've just forgotten! All you have to do now is to make the chat look intimate.

But I loved it and working with Mary was just such a pleasure. In fact, one of my particular pleasures was making her laugh. It wasn't difficult. She would generally be on the edge anyway and a gentle push would have her away. One of my favourites was when she was reading a piece directly to the camera and all I'd have to do was walk behind the camera and wave at her. Just for a bit of diversion, I would sometimes wave something of the food variety from Neven's selection. I particularly favoured artichokes and perhaps an unusually shaped piece of ginger. It rarely failed and the trick then, as the break began, was to slip out of the studio before she caught me.

The show had another side to it, because stories about families, about illnesses, about loss would also feature. The lady who brought us these was one of the finest researchers I ever worked with, Liz Feely. She just had an instinct for a good story and a story that would lend itself to 10 or more minutes of TV. She just seem to be able to gauge what we would get from somebody through her exhaustive research and constantly delivered the most perfect guests. At times it could be difficult because we were dealing with real-life issues, with somebody who is live on television, as opposed to radio, so there was nowhere to hide. For anybody who had never been on television before this was quite a daunting prospect. But it worked, and much of that has to be down to Liz's ability to make people comfortable and to convince them that we weren't out to get them, but in fact, were there to bring out their story to the best of our ability. I hope we did them some justice.

When it comes to 'celebrities', everybody sat on that couch, from Brendan O'Carroll to Eddie Izzard! Two lads unafraid of ladies' garments. There were many more. We had quite a selection of authors come through and one of my favourites was the late, great Pete McCarthy. He was responsible for a phenomenal book called *McCarthy's Bar*, the true story of one man's journey from Cork to Donegal, where the travel adage, 'Never pass a bar that has your name on it,' was used to great effect. Any book about Ireland that can link Michael Collins, Jimi Hendrix and St Patrick's Purgatory has to have something going for it. His follow-on book, *The Road to McCarthy* was just as madcap. Now, he was travelling the world in search of an hereditary Gaelic chief and I remember one snippet, where he met a man in a bar and decided that the McCarthy clan had come to Ireland from North Africa, and had been subjected to a 'rusting process', where the damp Irish weather had broken down their natural pigment, so that over time, they ended up with red hair and freckles. We laughed our way through the interview and it's been my intention whenever I get a chance to go away on a really decent break to bring both books with me because I'll simply giggle the time away.

Another favourite was our very own sports commentator, Jimmy Magee, who remembers everything, and if I try to catch him out, I can't. I remember a story – not sure if it's true – about a group of lads being away for an international football game and they met Jimmy Magee in the square of the town. The first fella, clearly the worse for drink, says to Jimmy, 'Is it true that you have a great memory, Jimmy, that you recall everything?'

Jimmy replies, 'So they say. What do you want to know?'

To which the fella says, 'What hotel are we staying in, Jimmy?'

We had specials of the show, too, where we would honour one person or group of people, like the Dubliners, for instance, or our Daniel O'Donnell special, where we had an invited audience in to watch the show. It was just like an evening entertainment programme and got really good audience figures. The shows required a lot of hard work from the team, but they always came up trumps, helped by the magic of the guest. You get that when you have people of a particular calibre in the studio: they elevate what you do to a new level, but you also see them surrounded by family and friends and there's a different aura about them; generally the warmer, calmer side of them is evident. Then, of course, there was the music, which was such a big part of the show. Just having the opportunity to sit on the couch with Chris Rea as he talked about the pancreatic cancer that nearly took him from us was very moving. He was one of the nicest, warmest human beings I've ever met. Of course, he comes from an old ice cream-making family of the Italian variety, the Reas of Middlesbrough. What a sweet man. Sorry, that just slipped out.*

Open House was just good telly thought through and brought to fruition by professionals; we were very lucky to work with people of this calibre and we were very lucky to have a terrific audience out there watching. You see, here is the thing about daytime television. There is a perception that it is for people who are older, or students, or the unemployed, as well as those at home who never stop working around the house. I found that the audience was all of these and many more, so catering for them could be a bit of a minefield. But that was the great thing about the programme: audience reaction. Viewers would get in touch almost immediately and let you know exactly what they thought of what you were doing, which was great. I'm such a believer that the viewer is a real living part of the show and when you mention them, they feel doubly so and it's that sense of family that makes something like *Open House* work as well as it did. I suppose it's really a bit like radio on the telly, because you come into people's lives

---

* But it does give me a chance to share an ice cream joke with you. I think this is from Tommy Cooper; 'So I went down to my local ice cream shop and said, "I want to buy an ice cream." He said, "Hundreds and thousands?" I said, "No, just the one."'

every day, you relate to them and they relate to you. We recap on yesterday's bits and pieces and today we're off on new adventures and stories and whatever comes our way, but the key is, we're doing it together. So that link is vital.

Sometimes, mind you, the audience response could be very funny. We used to do items about nutritious foods, you know, things like lentils and pulses and all that and more than once, I can tell you, I was stopped on the street and told something like, 'Would you not get that one to have a decent meal and stop annoying me with her nuts and seeds.' Nobody meant any harm or criticism, but because they were a part of the show every day, they felt they could tell us things. That's the great thing about television, or at least one of them: people can say what they like to you. I frequently had comments like, 'What were you doing in that tie?' You'd think I had nothing else on!

The response that used to amuse me in particular was about make-up. Not mine, the ladies' make-up. Various beauty experts would come in and share their tips about mascara, foundation or make-up tones for spring and autumn, things I wouldn't have the first notion about, but because we were on TV, everyone was an expert. Now, there are experts and experts! It seemed to me that no matter what these experts did, it was never good enough and I'd hear things like, 'Anyway, did you see the state of your one in the white coat? She is no oil painting, I can tell you, and she's giving advice! No thanks, love, I'll be grand.' But again always with a lot of goodwill. It was all just about the banter. Sure, even the then Lord Mayor,

Royston Brady, bestowed an award of the Dublin variety on Mary and me when the series ended. We are very big in City Hall, you know. Ask anyone.

...

But back to Jimmy Webb. When it transpired that he was going to play in Dublin, I nearly had apoplexy. The great Peter Aiken was bringing him in and he was prepared to come in to *Open House* and have the chat: sometimes, as the fella said, you'd be lost for words. I was actually going to sit and chat with one of my all-time musical heroes and there was always the possibility of a piano being wheeled in if I could get Christy on the job with the big muscles on him.

Now, you might ask who the great Jimmy Webb is. Why, amongst my list of song-writing heroes sits this son of Oklahoma and explainer in song of so much of my teenage dreams. He's a bit like myself, an old romantic, but that's good. For years, I had followed his career, obviously back in those heady days in the sixties when he wrote absolute classics like 'MacArthur Park', a huge hit for Richard Harris and, later, Donna Summer, and 'Galveston', 'By the Time I Get to Phoenix', and my favourite, 'Wichita Lineman', for Glen Campbell. I fell in love with Jimmy Webb's music even before I knew there was a Jimmy Webb, the man behind those classic songs. But when the seventies rolled round, I was introduced to the music of the man himself by a bouncer pal at the Grove (remember that?), Denny McGrath, a man of impeccable taste. I discovered his less well-known work on albums like *Words and Music*,

And So On, Letters, Land's End and my favourite, *El Mirage*, the last one produced by the great George Martin, he of the relatively successful Liverpool combo.

I immediately fell in love with Webb's music. He wrote songs that told of heartbreak, of hope for love, songs about his career, but always with this beautiful melody. He had an ability to make a small band sound like an orchestra and the words were pure poetry. There's a song on the album, 'If You See Me Getting Smaller, I'm Leaving', which tells a story of a musician with a borderline career and evokes so beautifully the loneliness of it all. The album also features the classic 'Highwayman', recorded by Johnny Cash, Roy Orbison *et al*. Oh, and by the way, if it's heartache you're after, have a listen to 'Where the Universes Are', another killer love song. All beauts and added to by the many songs written by him and covered by Art Garfunkel, Linda Ronstadt, Carly Simon and more. It was Jimmy's plaintive voice that got to me, the singer singing his own song, feeling it, living it. With all the music that's out there, it's very easy for someone who isn't storming the charts to get forgotten, to get lost in the rush and to be cast aside. The thing about Jimmy is, he refuses to go away, a bit like myself. He may not be the world's number-one download, but I'd much rather spend an evening listening to him than attempting to twerk to Miley Cyrus! To be honest, that's liable to have me back out!

Well, when the day duly arrived (don't call me Julie) I was so excited I don't think I had any food all morning and just paced around the place like a man with ants in his pants.

And you know what, it was just as I had expected; this fine fella turned out to be as I'd hoped. I'd brought along all my vinyl LPs as I suspected I might be one of very few people to have the lot in Ireland. It transpires I was kind of right, although I subsequently discovered an elite group of us who all love his music. But he graciously sat down in his dressing room, signed the albums and talked about each one with a fondness that proved to me how important they were in his life and how much it meant that somebody loved them enough to bring them to him to sign. We must have chatted for ages in the dressing room before he came on for the sort of chat that television doesn't give you enough time to share with the viewer – because you know that most people aren't familiar with the songs and just want to hear the big hits – but for me it was a moment set in stone and I'll never forget it. I was so caught in the conversation that time ran away with me and extra minutes were added to the show. But it was great and at the end of it he offered to sing and off with him to the piano, where he launched into 'Wichita Lineman' live in the studio. It had to be one of the most incredible moments for me on TV.*

✳ Which reminds me ... Dr Mooney was on the radio show again with this gem: A young man was walking through Sherwood Forest in the early morning and came upon Robin Hood resting under the spreading branches of an old oak tree. 'Good morning young fellow,' says Robin. 'How are you on this fine spring morning?' 'Very well, thank you,' answers the young man. 'How would you like to join my band?' asks Robin. 'I would love to,' answers the young man and immediately runs into Nottingham and buys a trombone. Thank you, Declan, for keeping the musical element alive.

Actually that was one of the important things about *Open House*. Having a musical element from time to time gave it the feel not only of a magazine programme but more of a variety programme and that was important. You weren't always going to get top-of-the-range singers and bands, but you would get very credible ones nonetheless and that made for a more rounded show. It also gave us the opportunity, when we were brainstorming in the office, to come up with musical specials, like the Dubliners, Daniel O'Donnell and others. These turned out not only to be excellent music shows but an opportunity for Mary and me to chat with these guests in front of an invited audience. Ah, great days.

That reminds me, when Daniel was on the show, his special, I was taken with how bright and funny he was, a clever man with a ready wit. (Which reminds me of that great Donegal comedian Conal Gallen and his song, 'Where Did All The Folk 'n' Ballad Singers Go?' Now, all you have to do here to get the full effect is to repeat that question quickly and then quicker again! Are you catching my drift?)

And then there were the Dubliners, a truly great act and now nearly all gone. I recall that they were in the charts when I was a small boy with a song called 'Seven Drunken Nights' – not a mention of a round table, by the way – and I've always enjoyed the story about the early days of the band: they were down the country playing a gig, and Ronnie had a proper job back in Dublin and needed to get home, so he gave the barman a fiver to close the bar. But it never happened. When they got home, he said to the lads: 'That barman was some chancer. Gave him a fiver to close the bar and he didn't.'

'Ah' says Barney, 'I gave him a tenner to keep it open.'

Add to that list Chris Rea, Deacon Blue, Nick Hayward and more local talent than you could shake a stick at and the musical world was well served by *Open House*. But therein lies the joy of a TV show that involves you and evolves, day by day, to become what you want it to become, essential viewing. Like *Countdown*, without the numbers round! If a TV show can become an appointment to watch, like *Open House* did, it becomes very much the fabric of people's days. In fact, many people (viewers, that is) worked around *Open House* so they wouldn't miss it. It wasn't unheard of for the shopping to be done and the evening meal prepared in the early afternoon, the cleaning to be sorted, so that people could sit down and really engage with the programme.

That's why it was such a shock when the powers that be decided it was time for it to go after six years. I've said it before and I'll say it again, in television this happens all the time and with some programmes, it's just the way of it. In television, change is often made for change's sake, or to keep ahead of the curve, and, as presenters, we just have to accept that. But it's hard when the show has formed a relationship with the viewer and vice versa. Then, it's a very different parting and *Open House* did not go quietly. Once there was an inkling that the show was going to end, the viewers started to protest, initially with phone calls to the show, and then they started to bombard the place. Letters of protest went to the papers; one paper, *The Sun*, even took up the cause and it became quite the campaign. But the writing was on the wall. When a decision is made about a programme and it's been concluded that something else is needed, there's not a lot you can do about it. Everything in the world of television is finite: some shows, particularly in America, don't even complete one season. Some get a second run out and that will be that, but we got six years with *Open House* and that's a good run.

I suppose if you're in the office making decisions, you might feel that it's time to get something shiny and new. The problem, however, with shiny and new is that it isn't always what you want because there is also a place for the less shiny; for the warm, the comfortable and, that much-maligned word, the familiar. The phrase goes that familiarity breeds contempt, but in our case, I think familiarity bred a contentment that the viewers did not want to let go of. Then we had the problem, of course, of presenting the show, knowing that it wasn't coming back. That's not the easiest thing in the world to do because you know that you should give it your best and yet you don't feel in the mood. Well, we did give our best shot, we gave it welly and aimed to make the best shows of our run and give it everything we had.

Of course, when a show like *Open House* ends, everybody on the production side moves on to another show, as it should be, because they have a talent which is proven and it's only right and proper that they continue to work away, but it's the poor old presenters who end up looking for the next gig. As I learned with Century, things go in cycles. It has worked out, thank God, even though at the time you're not sure how it will. All you can do in my position is to be ready for the next move and grasp it with both hands when it comes. It's true that when a great show like *Open House* ends, it concentrates the mind. I feel that doing my best is always important, but surviving at some level is vital. If you see your livelihood being taken away from you, then that's where your resilience, sense of purpose and, most important, self-belief is tested. You need that self-belief in my business and I'm very lucky that my parents instilled that in me. I don't know what it was but at the time I just felt something would come from this, I suppose it's simply self-belief, and I'd been here before, more than once. And it turned out to be the case with my aforementioned relationship with the Lottery. This career may have its ups and downs, but it's the only one for me.

I think it's time to hear from one of my radio regulars to bring a bit of cheer here. Ken told us a story about Jack Lemmon and his friendship with Walter Matthau. They were filming a scene in which Walter was coming down a flight of stairs, but he slipped and fell heavily, landing on his back at the foot of the stairs. Concerned, Jack ran over to his friend and asked, 'Walt, are you comfortable?' Matthau opened one eye, shrugged his shoulders and said, 'I make a living.' You gotta laugh. Sometimes that's all that is left to you.

The purpose of this little interlude is to say that I didn't want to be downhearted about the ending of *Open House*. I didn't want them to knock me down. It's difficult when your self-belief is questioned, but I was lucky enough to have people around me who knew that I am good at what I do. I suppose it's about the whole issue of change again and having some voice in that change. Who moved your cheese and all that. Once in a while it would be lovely to move your own cheese, but that prospect is often out of our reach in this TV world; our betters will decide and there it rests.

But let me tell you that being prepared isn't always the way and quite often you're not. Happily for me at the time people in radio were watching this with interest. It transpired that there were those who felt that this worked well on TV. Mary's gone on to something else, Marty worked in radio back in the day, why not harvest this and bring him back to the wireless ... Bliss. That's the thing about change, I suppose, you never know when it's going to happen or where it'll take you. In my case, it took me back to my first love, radio. It began with Derek Mooney (of *Mooney Goes Wild* fame), who was producing the Special Olympics and approached me to commentate. I was thrilled, and so, after 12 years, found myself broadcasting on RTÉ radio again. Through Derek, the spell was broken.

But let me leave the final word on change to a Mr Power, who got in touch with *Marty in the Morning* one morning from Lhasa in Tibet. He told me about the time the Dalai Lama ordered a €10 pizza and paid with a €20 note. The pizza guy put the note in the till and closed it and the Dalai Lama said, 'Where's my change?' The pizza guy replied: 'Change comes from within.'

'Heroes'

David Bowie

The *Collins English Dictionary* defines a hero as 'a man distinguished by exceptional courage, nobility, fortitude, etc.' Or, more precisely, 'a man who is idealized for possessing superior qualities in any field'. (Surely in this day and age a hero can be a woman? Come on, girls, what about Meryl Streep or Aung San Suu Kyi, or Mary Robinson, or ... anyway, there's lots of them.) The point is, we all need heroes. According to Richard Davenport Hines in a recent issue of *The Oldie* magazine (what am I doing, just approaching middle age, reading a magazine like that? It must be preparation for advanced age, which is way down the line.) Those who look up to someone as a model – whether a relation, a sporting hero, or a singer – tend to the good. Those who never learned to admire go to the bad. True or not, I have no idea, but I do like a hero.

'Why so?' I hear you cry. Perhaps having heroes makes not one jot of difference. Maybe one way or the other, we turn out to be the people we are simply because of how we are reared, or the company we keep, the sort of circles we move in (preferably concentric ones, but then, you knew that). The other thing is the danger that your hero or heroine turns out to have feet of clay. But that should not matter at all, because let's face it, you're hero-worshipping them on your terms, not theirs, at least I hope so.

Working in radio and television gives you access to all manner of people, some wonderful beyond compare, and some – how shall I put this politely – some you can't wait to see the back of, because quite frankly, the front of them wasn't much fun either. You see, there are those who enter a radio or TV studio and change into a persona, not always that of the person you thought you were going to meet. Strangely, the bigger the name the less they are inclined to do so. Being a hero isn't about being famous, but about possessing those exceptional qualities Mr Collins talks about above. A true hero is just like the rest of us, just doing what we do and not inclined to give anybody any bother at all. I would look to my dad as one of my heroes, but not in a 'heroic' way. He was actually a very simple and straightforward man – he wasn't strident or bombastic or full of ambition. He was very happy with his lot. He saw it as his role in life to look after me and Mam and to keep us in comfort, which he did, but he wanted me to do as well as I could. He wouldn't push, he'd just encourage, and praise when things had gone well, but not admonish when they hadn't. He might just say, 'That's a pity,' but nothing more. He let me work things out.

He was also a lovely warm man – we hugged always, and we'd talk for Ireland. He was great company and I think I was rarely happier when I was younger than when there were just the two of us, having a conversation. He was a great man for advice and a great man for the quip (No, not a quiff. He lost his hair when he was in his twenties, for heaven's sake.) I miss him still. But we maintained a glorious relationship until the day he died: we never fell out, never had an argument that didn't end quickly and all my memories of him are positive. Just a wonderful, warm dad. The sort that songs are written about, or should be.

During my brief career as a drummer, he drove me around to whatever gig we played and waited patiently outside to bring me home again, but he wouldn't have been the most ardent supporter of my decision to leave the security of a career in insurance to move into broadcasting; in fact, he was convinced I was bonkers, stark raving mad. He couldn't quite fathom how you could leave a permanent pensionable job for one year's contract in a career that might not last any longer than that year. Perceptive in his own way, I suppose, but we're still standing, proper job or no. (Which reminds me of the joke: 'I had thought about becoming an historian but there's no future in it!' Suit yourself.)

My dad was and is a hero to me, not really because he did anything monumental – he didn't save people in far-off lands, or go to the moon, but what he did was mind my mother and me and cherish us in a way that I hope I've been able to do with my own family. If he taught me anything, it's that you can be a hero just by doing these simple things as well. By being a good person.

...

Fortitude is one of the qualities of a hero, according to Mr Collins, as well as those superior qualities 'in any field'. The world of entertainment is full of people who keep going, for whom longevity is the thing. And because of that they become household names through the generations: in music, that could be Van Morrison, Burt Bacharach, Paul McCartney and Barbra Streisand, or as one of my listeners likes to call her, Barbara Streisland! In politics, Garret FitzGerald, John Hume, Michael D. Higgins. In writing, it's Seamus Heaney for poetry, it's Bob Woodward for American politics, Larry Gogan for the fine-tuned link in the world of radio and so on. (What is it about Larry and the 'Just a Minute' quiz? The man is a living legend and the quiz with him. He really is the best company. I spent many a happy Eurovision traipsing the streets of Europe with him in search of a little local colour for the broadcast. But more of the Eurovision later; it deserves its own section because, quite frankly, it truly is its own world and no mistake.) They all have a certain something in common: exceptional talent; and they just keep on going, year after year. But let's look at some of these people in terms of the hero within.

All through the years I have loved comedy, which some of you may have noticed. I don't just mean jokes; I mean funny sentences, plays on words, limericks, all of that. Now, I was far too young to remember the Goons the first time round, that comic *tour de force* of Harry Secombe, Spike Milligan, Peter Sellers and Michael Bentine. After all, I was only four, hardly old enough to have finished nibbling on bits of Liga. It wasn't until much later that I teamed up with my best pal from school, Leo of the Conways, late of Stiles Road, Clontarf, that the Goons entered my life. After Belgrove National School in Clontarf, I'd moved to St Paul's in Raheny for first year, which was then called prep school. This was a clever move on my parents' part, because being in first year meant that unless you were a complete eejit and learnt absolutely nothing, you really couldn't fail the entrance exam to the secondary school itself, which began in second year. So I was in and Leo was me pal. The instant attraction between Leo and me was marvellous: both of us loved music, both of us had bikes, both of us had no interest whatsoever in football and neither of us could get over the bar in the pole vault in the gym. We knew our limitations and were happy to share them with everybody. Leo, having two older brothers, Peter and James, had taken his influences from them. It really was quite cosmopolitan down on Stiles Road, you know ... I'm talking about jazz music and the Goons. While everybody else seemed to be listening to Uriah Heep and Black Sabbath, Leo and I would be enjoying the restrained guitarist Wes Montgomery and early

George Benson, with perhaps a little bit of Weather Report. If we'd had the ability to grow a little beard, we would have obliged. Leo's oldest brother James was a Goon fan and as a result had LPs of the stuff. So that was the beginning of my love affair with the Goons. We rolled around the place as the gags came thick and fast – wonderful memories. And as the Goons was written largely by Spike Milligan, he quickly became a hero.

Over the years, I have devoured every book he published: his war memoirs, his reworking of classic books, his books of poetry and his classic novel *Puckoon*, set in a fictional village in Sligo – a work of genius. Here's a line: '"Darling," he whined – "you know full well dere's no work round dese parts," and he pointed as far as the fence', or the passage about the character Dan Milligan's legs:

> 'Legs.'
> 'Legs? LEGS? Whose legs?'
> 'Yours.'
> 'Mine? And who are you?'
> 'The author.'
> 'Author? Author? Did you write these legs?'
> 'Yes.'
> 'Well, I don't like dem. I don't like 'em at all at all. I could ha' writted better legs meself. Did you write your legs?'
> 'No.'
> 'Ahhh. *Sooo*! You got someone else to write your legs, someone who's a good leg writer and den you

write dis pair of crappy old legs fer me, well mister,
it's not good enough.'

You can see where this is heading, daft as a box of frogs
and all the better for it. I was hooked, line and sinker. And
before I proceed with the point of our exercise, a limerick:

A combustible woman from Thang,
Exploded one day with a bang,
The maid then rushed in,
And said with a grin,
'Pardon me Madam – you rang?'

Ah, yes, I feel much better now and at least it's out of me
system.

...

As I mentioned previously, in the mid-nineties I found myself
presenting a TV show called *Off the Record,* the idea being
that we would invite celebrities in, interview them and, inter-
spersed with that, the RTÉ Concert Orchestra, a fine body
of men and women then and now, would play some of their
favourite music. The series was produced by my friend of
many years and colleague Ian McGarry (funnily enough also
a drummer and also, wait for it, an only child). With all
manner of fine guests passing through, it turned out to be a
really enjoyable series; in fact, we got a second run the following year. Word came that Spike Milligan had agreed to
come over from London and be in the show. Now, I can't
begin to tell you how excited I was, so I won't bother.

The day of the recording arrived and the car was duly sent to collect Spike from the hotel. It was only when he arrived in the dressing room that it was discovered he'd come over a day early and spent the time in his hotel room, which didn't bode well. Fan that I was, I met him in the dressing room before the show armed with my 16 books and whatever other bits of Spike Milligan and Goon memorabilia I could muster. He seemed pleased. I was pleased he was pleased. So, the ice was broken and off we went to make the programme. The only problem was, he wasn't really in the best of form. The trouble with Spike was that he was either very high or very low: you never knew until the day which Spike would turn up. It subsequently transpired that he had been suffering from bipolar disorder for much of his life and had had quite a few nervous breakdowns. Obviously, he was on medication and the upshot of all this was that you either had him on a high high or a low low, but in the early stage of our interview, he seemed far more intent on a bit of one-upmanship than being the wonderful guest I knew he could be; but then, after a bit of this to-ing and fro-ing, he suddenly turned into the perfect guest: he told stories, made us laugh and, overall, was a joy. It was interesting to see how many members of the orchestra stayed in their positions to listen to him, enthralled. He was and remains a huge influence on me, and the fact that I got to meet and spend a little time with somebody I had so admired for so many years was such a privilege.

I, of course, was not the only one to have a certain trepidation about interviewing Spike Milligan. I recall Jonathan

Ross when he was on Channel 4 back in the day, interviewing Spike live and it getting absolutely nowhere. Jonathan turned to the camera and said; 'Please God, take me now.' It says it all. But I love him to this day and so many of his quotes and gags and limericks come into my mind daily on the radio, like this one: 'A sure cure for seasickness is to sit under a tree,' and, 'All I ask is the chance to prove that money can't make me happy.' Now that is a hero in any man's language.

Spike Milligan died in 2002 and his gravestone famously reads: '*Dúirt me leat go raibh mé breoite*', because he wasn't allowed to use the English translation: 'I told you I was sick'. He made me laugh for years and still does, but he also made me think, because he was a clever guy and cared passionately about many things ... but I will always remember him for being as daft as a brush.

...

The Collins' definition definitely applies to other heroes I've met, unsung in many ways and getting on with life. On *Open House*, we met so many incredible people. People you might never hear of, parents of children who had been injured or who had died, people who had lost livelihoods and subsequently their homes and told us their stories, honest and true. We met wonderful people who had overcome tragedy, moved on with their lives and had attempted, as best they could, to carry on and fight the good fight. These people are in many ways the real heroes because so often they quietly deal with what they must.

Can you imagine somebody coming on television and sitting with us and telling us their story accompanied by their child, who might have been greatly disabled, unable to speak or do the normal things that children do? This is the family turned upside down by circumstance and yet doing their best to cope. Why? Love, that's why and, indeed, how. I suppose that is what prompted Mary and me to become patrons of the Carers Association, to try to support them in any way possible and to get their story out into the media. It's the story of thousands of people in this country, some of whom are actually only children, who take on the task of caring for family members, old and young. These are the real unsung heroes and we met them on *Open House* time and again.

But when I think further about heroes, I think about people who really mattered to us when we were growing up, and high in that firmament was one David Bowie. I remember, back in the mid-seventies, going to the Grove and all the great music that Cecil would play. He was the great DJ at the Grove. Gorgeous man and very caring. I remember he went off to America once and he asked me if there were any albums I'd like him to look out for me. So I have Cecil to thank for my American pressing of Van Morrison's *Wavelength* album and a few more. Decent man, Cecil.

But back to David Bowie. It was the music, it was the style, it was the attitude, it was the sense of danger about him, from New York to Berlin and back. Even now, as I think back to songs like 'Jean Genie', or 'Drive-in Saturday', or

'Life on Mars' or 'Heroes' even, the name of the bloomin' chapter. He was magic, not that we dressed like him or anything, it's just that the music was so incredible. Nobody else made music like he did. Every time I hear it brings you right back to the Grove and those innocent days. Of course, we all went out then and bought albums with titles like *The Rise and Fall of Ziggy Stardust and the Spiders from Mars* and *Aladdin Sane*.

Some years later, in the early eighties, I was working on the *Video File* series, which, as you will recall, involved an interview of, say, 20 minutes with a visiting music star. We would intersperse the edited interview with four videos and, hey presto, you had a TV show. When word came through that we had been granted an interview with David Bowie, we just couldn't believe it. The amazing thing was that he was playing at Slane in Co. Meath and, rather than do an interview sometime before the gig and obviously help promote it and sell tickets, he decided to do the interview at Slane before the gig happened. Mad or what. So, off we trekked with our film crew, led by a fearless Mr Bil Keating and accompanied by Mrs Whelan, who wasn't going to miss this opportunity, I can assure you of that! We set up our little group on the banks of the Boyne, me a nervous wreck, because getting the chance to spend a quarter of an hour with somebody of the calibre of David Bowie was very special and rare indeed.

After a short wait, he ambled over to us, greeted every member of the crew and sat down, while all around him mayhem abounded. The camera rolled and we chatted and we chatted, not a bother. He did notice at one stage that the sunlight was playing havoc in his eyes, so he suggested we stop filming and I thought, that's that then. But no, we changed position and off we went again. As the interview was going along, very nicely, I thought I could sense the hovering of his PR person, who went and walked behind him and started making motions to wrap up the interview. I gently nodded, but continued (that's the Northside Dubliner in me). Funny thing is, Bowie paused and gestured to the PR to leave us, that we were fine and we'd continue talking until we had concluded our piece. What amazed me was that he said he was really enjoying the chat and didn't want to stop until we got what we needed.

Now in my estimation, with some of the eejits I've had to endure over the years, this was a real star being a bit of a gent, and he's been a hero of mine ever since. Please note in the photograph that Mr Bowie and Mr Whelan are smiling at the camera; note, however, where Mrs Whelan is looking, who she is smiling at and who she's holding on to. Maybe it was the sunshine, maybe it was the wonderful aroma wafting from the River Boyne, maybe – no, it was definitely David Bowie.

Another star who turned out to be really, really nice was Phil Collins. To interview him, we went over to Genesis/Phil Collins's recording studio outside London and, typical of us, we went over when it was snowing. I am reliably informed that this was 1989. Now, remember this is the guy who for the Live Aid concerts in 1985 had played in Wembley and then, thanks to Concorde, had played in Philadelphia on the same day, and he was also the guy who was never off the radio. So I didn't know what to expect when I met him for the first of three occasions. I needn't have worried. The first thing he did on greeting us was to put on the kettle and make us tea. Not only did he do a superb interview but he allowed us to mess around in his studio and, considering that Ian McGarry and myself both profess to be able to play the drums, can you imagine how starstruck we were? Another day in paradise.*

Now, you may not know this, but I love my politics and read up on it all the time. Not just Irish politics, but UK and US politics in particular. We'll cover that again later, but while we're on the subject of heroes – steady now, hang on to something, here we go – with the thousands and thousands of politicians over the years, there have to be a few good ones in there that make a difference. There sits at the top of everybody John Hume, a man who embodies the definition of being a hero. John Hume, of course, from Derry in Northern Ireland, a founder of the Social Democratic and Labour Party and indeed its leader from 1979 until 2001. In terms of Northern Ireland history he is, without question, one of its most important leaders and was a great believer in peaceful protest and the civil rights

---

* What's this they say about drummers? Oh yes. What do you call someone who hangs around with musicians? Answer: a drummer. Yeah, yeah, yeah.

of everyone. His heroes were Gandhi and Martin Luther King Jr and it's fitting that he went and won the Gandhi Peace Prize, the Martin Luther King Jr Award and shared the Nobel Peace Prize with David Trimble in 1998. This is a man who has made a huge contribution to our island. That was the thing about him, he always spoke about our divided people and his efforts to bring us together. And you have to say to yourself, no matter what, just how different would things in the North be had there not been a John Hume. Of course, we'll never know, but I am convinced that his involvement, his dedication, his fearlessness, his belief in a better way and his hard work to achieve it was instrumental in the peace that reigns today.

I was fortunate enough to interview him for *Off the Record,* the very same show on which I'd interviewed Spike Milligan. Interviewing John Hume was a joy, because his ability to speak with such passion washed over you. You knew that he knew what he wanted to say and how he would articulate it. You would ask him a question and sit back and enjoy the answer. While we did have plenty of political guests on the show, *Off the Record* wasn't a programme to push or cajole somebody about their politics. It was all about giving them a platform to give a sense of the person. With John Hume, personal stuff came into the conversation, how each day was lived, how special occasions were celebrated, what it was like when, as a member of the European Parliament, he was able to address them in fluent French. He was just a really interesting man who had made such a difference and who was comfortable in his own skin, explaining his point of view and his hopes for a brighter future for us all. If there has to be one political hero, for me it has to be John Hume. Actually, if you want to read a book about John Hume, can I just recommend *John Hume: A Statesman of the Troubles*, by Barry White.* (Oh, for heaven's sake, no, not the Walrus of Love – what are you like?)

I've been asked a few times if I would get into politics. A number of individuals from various parties have approached me in a chatty sort of way to suss me out. I wasn't for sussing. Much as I love to read about it, and the number of books I possess on politics is testament to that, I couldn't imagine politics as a career for me. Quite frankly, I wouldn't be a great man for banging on doors, clutching my manifesto as I go; sore thing on a windy day, you know! But all this does remind me of my favourite political joke, from a *Marty in the Morning* listener with his or her finger on the American pulse: former president George W. Bush went into Burger King and asked the server for two whoppers, to which the guy replied: 'You're an intellectual giant and the best president we ever had.'**

...

*   Blackstaff Press, Belfast 1984.

**   And the other one I love is about the weather being really, really cold, so cold that numerous politicians have actually been seen with their hands in their own pockets!

Another US president who absolutely fascinates me is Richard Milhous Nixon. A flawed character, certainly, but as time has passed, allowing me to get a sense of who he was and what he was about, not everything is a negative. All we hear about always is Watergate, but this president was also responsible for the enforced desegregation of schools in the southern US, for reforming healthcare and social welfare, for opening diplomatic relations with the Chinese in 1972, for a *détente* with the Soviet Union; and he became an elder statesman and was a foreign policy expert into his dotage. Actually, a few years ago I visited his family home in Yorba Linda, California, and paid my respects at his grave. What was that quote I learned at school? 'The bad men do lives after them, the good is oft interred with their bones.' I bet you that's Shakespeare – *Julius Caesar*, to be precise.

Yes, Nixon did wrong and paid with the ending of his career, but I also remember a couple of amazing quotes of his: 'Remember, always give your best. Never get discouraged. Never be petty. Always remember, others may hate you. But those who hate you don't win unless you hate them. And then you destroy yourself.' Powerful stuff. And the other quote has also had a profound effect on me: 'Only if you have been in the deepest valley, can you ever know how magnificent it is to be on the highest mountain.' See what I mean? Love him or loathe him, he was fascinating and remains so for me. As the years have passed there are more and more questions being asked about how Watergate happened in the first place. Maybe we'll never get the answer, just like the JFK assassination; now don't get me started on that!

I think it's time for a good gag now, maybe one about politics, something like, 'A politician has to be able to see both sides of an issue, so he can get around it.'

And now, on to movie stars … Actors, a fine breed of men and women who, in some cases, take themselves terribly seriously. I love Bob Hope's line from one Oscar ceremony. He presented 19 times, but in 1968 he issued the immortal line: 'I've never seen six hours whiz by so fast'! I would have great time for Spencer Tracy of *Father of the Bride* and *Guess Who's Coming to Dinner?* fame, and Edward G. Robinson, who played the gangster in countless movies, both greats from my father's time. I have huge admiration and fondness for the great Alastair Sim – in fact, with Margaret Rutherford, he starred in my favourite film of all time, *The Happiest Days of Your Life*, about a school evacuation during World War Two which goes badly wrong, with hilarious results. It was made six years before I was born, but to this day I adore Alastair Sim and Margaret Rutherford and there's nothing quite like a rainy Thursday around two in the afternoon with a large bar of Cadbury's milk chocolate and one of their old movies to enjoy.

But I digress, as usual, because my great hero in the world of acting is Al Pacino. An only boy and one of the finest actors known the world over. I've been collecting his films on video for years (I know, quaintly old-fashioned, but no matter where I am in the world, I go on the Al Pacino hunt and generally find something new.) I suppose it goes back to that period when he was making really unusual films like *Dog Day Afternoon* about a bank robber funding his wife's sex-change operation, and the *Godfather* trilogy, as well as the comedy, *Author, Author,* about a stressed-out playwright and his family, and the courtroom drama, *And Justice for All.* Right through all of those, and on to his Oscar for *Scent of a Woman,* I just knew he was my favourite.

So, what happened only the Philosophical Society at Trinity College Dublin decided to invite him in and present him with an award. Now, not having the third level under me oxter, I had absolutely no right to assume I'd have any chance of going and seeing him, but this marvellous girl, a colleague from the newsroom had access to a ticket and … guess what? She offered the ticket to me and, of course, being the gentleman I am, I immediately said that I couldn't possibly accept such a hugely sought-after prize … no, I didn't. I grabbed the ticket with both hands, leapt into the air with excitement and said, 'Yes, yes, yes, thank you, thank you, thank you.'

Seriously now, I couldn't sleep, I was actually like a child, waiting for the Big Day. Like a One Direction nut or someone hanging on every syllable of Ed Sheeran's warblings! In I went, got a seat around the middle of the hall, because I was early, and the place filled up. After a while, various academics arrived and got seated in the appropriate sections and then came the arrival of the great man …

'Who-ha ...' as his character, Frank Slade, said in *Scent of a Woman*. Pacino gave a talk from the lectern, he recited some Shakespeare and he was awe-inspiring. My friend and colleague, Ryan Tubridy, did a Q&A and then it was over. At this point everyone was preparing to leave and among our number were some faces I knew, including the great director of the Gate Theatre, Michael Colgan. We'd chatted and nodded to each other during Al Pacino's appearance, like two old thespians smiling approval at a third colleague. Michael seemed to have access to the inner sanctum so we shoved forward with the crowd and in the time-honoured way, Michael gave the security man the old 'he's with me' number. I appreciated his willingness to include me in the move as we shuffled forward. It worked, I was in. The only problem with this plan was that various gowned fellows decided to nab me to have a chat with me about the Lotto and radio and Daz ads and whatever. All I wanted was to get to Al Pacino and say hello – 'who-ha'! What I was going to say I had no idea, but I had the trusty camera with me and you may as well go for it, I thought.

Between the jigs and the reels, I eventually made my way over to where our diminutive friend was (not that I told him he seemed smaller in reality: this was Al Pacino, for pity's sake. Did you see him in *Scarface*? Do I look like the brave type?). Suddenly, almost without warning, I found myself standing in front of my hero for decades. Now, remember at this stage in my career I had interviewed presidents, prime ministers, the biggest music stars, all manner of the great and the good, so it would be no bother to me. I went to open my mouth and nothing came out. Well, that's not technically true: air came out, accompanied by a dry mouth. With the dry mouth and the exhalation of air, my brain went into some kind of panic, because all I could muster were the words, 'I have all your fillums and I love them.'

All I wanted was for the earth to open up and swallow me, but because I was in front of my celluloid hero, I went for it a bald-headed and asked for a photo. He smiled, shook my hand, told me it was a pleasure to meet me (so, a better actor than even I had hoped) and posed for the picture. We exchanged some more pleasantries, but others, having seen me with the camera, were now feeling terribly brave and started to descend on our hapless hero. He was whisked away by the eager beavers and I stood there, rooted to the spot, but thrilled. Point is, he had done the polite thing, obviously realising, not for the first time, I'm sure, that he has such an effect on people and there are a few of us who are rendered speechless in his presence. I should have felt like a total dork and yet I didn't, because the thrill of meeting him was seeing that he was a decent human being with a capacity to understand the effect he could have on others. Very impressive.

...

Al Pacino mattered to me in a way that no other living actor did and all it would have taken was a swift brush-off and I would have been deflated beyond belief. You hear stories of people meeting their heroes and being completely let down, treated like nobody should ever be treated, because the hero turns out to have feet of clay. It's been suggested that my great musical hero Frank Sinatra was not the warmest of men and yet he did an incredible amount of good for people whom he never even met. He undoubtedly had a capacity for the darker side and he wasn't just the friendly person portrayed on all those wonderful albums from the Capitol Records Building and those marvellous reprise recordings. I haven't met him but I've read and read about Frank Sinatra and in my estimation, he errs on the side of being a good guy. His charity work raised millions all around the world; his kindness to strangers and friends alike is legendary, and if you did him a favour, he never forgot it.

Maria and I had the joy of a trip to New York recently and I was determined to go to a particular restaurant: an Italian place that from the outside doesn't look like anything spectacular at all; it's just a typical family-run Italian restaurant. It's called Patsy's, its location is West 56th Street in New York, and there's a story about this place. I got the story from Sal Scognamillo, who is co-owner and third-generation executive chef at the restaurant, which was founded by his grandfather in 1944. The story goes that, in the good years, Frank Sinatra, his wife Nancy and their children would go to Patsy's for dinner whenever they were in New York. He also brought in lots of friends like Jimmy Cagney, Dean Martin, Rosemary Clooney, on and on. Sometimes Frank would even go into the kitchen and cook alongside the owner. Now, there was a period when things were not exactly going well for Sinatra and one night he was having dinner alone. It was the day before Thanksgiving and Frank asked the owner what time they were serving the following night; 'I'll have dinner here with you guys.'

The things is, Patsy's didn't open on Thanksgiving, but the owner, realising that Sinatra was in a very lonely place, simply said, 'Three o'clock, Frank.'

'Great, see you then.'

The owner of Patsy's then called all the staff together and told them they would be open the following day. The deal was that they could bring their families to the restaurant for Thanksgiving dinner. And so it happened, and I'm sure Frank felt better for the fact that he was in company, with the Scognamillo family around him and a full and busy restaurant.

The point of this story is that when things were good, Sinatra had brought people to the restaurant and so, when things were not good, they looked out for him and went beyond the call of duty. To hear the story recounted by Sal that evening about his father and that relationship and to see the pride he took in retelling the tale let me know that his dad was a hero to him. You see, sometimes the hero's right beside you.

But if I was to pick one hero in all the world it would have to be Martin Luther King Jr. Now, that's a man I wish I had met, but through his writings and my favourite book of all time, a biography of Dr King called *Let the Trumpet Sound*, I can take myself to his world. It's not a world I would have found easy to inhabit, mind, at that time, but he was certainly a man whose company I'd want to keep. The very same man who issued the immortal line, 'Hatred and bitterness can never cure the disease of fear; only love can do that. Hatred paralyses life; love releases it. Hatred confuses life; love harmonises it. Hatred darkens life; love illuminates it.' When I take myself from the year of his assassination right up to my trip to Washington with my friend John Masterson to attend the inauguration of Barack Obama on 20 January 2009, and to see black faces all around me, particularly those of an older generation in tears at what was unfolding, it's easy to understand the connection that exists between Dr King and the people who voted for President Obama. The opportunity to be there on that day, and to witness such a momentous event will stay with me all my days. The slogan 'Yes We Can' made sense to me that day. It could well be a motto for life. After you've convinced yourself that it's possible all you have to do is convince everybody else around you, just as Martin Luther King Jr did all those years ago. Then change possible into probable.

To me, Martin Luther King sums up all the qualities of a hero: fortitude, courage and exceptional gifts. A man who wasn't afraid to stand up for what he believed in and to do it peacefully. Now, there's a hero. And in our complicated world, we need people who make us want to be better than ourselves, whether personally or professionally, people we can really look up to.

THE SPECIAL YEARS

'The Special Years'

Val Doonican

Before I had Jessica and Thomas, no one could have explained to me just how incredible it would be to have children. Of course, I had cousins with children, in-laws with children, friends with children, but we had none of our own. And then it happened with the arrival of Jessica in September 1990. I know it reads like a cliché, but it's true: your world turns completely upside down in a most unexpected way. You find yourself looking at this brand-new baby and all you want to do is protect it for the rest of your life. Isn't that unconditional love just something? The moment she arrived I knew nothing would ever be the same again.

Maria found herself in hospital sometime before our baby arrived, really as a precaution because of high blood pressure. I had been doing the best I could in the cause of Century Radio and had taken myself to bed on this particular day, having worked down the country the previous night. I need to explain something about me and bed: we are mad about each other. When I've read for a while, taken a last sip of water, turned out the light and put my head on the pillow, I tend to fall asleep in under six seconds and, to be honest, an earthquake wouldn't wake me. A fact I proved on our *Winning Streak* National Lottery trip to San Francisco that I mentioned in an earlier chapter.

So, it's the afternoon and I'm having a well-deserved rest, fully cognisant, of course, of the fact that Maria is in hospital and expecting our baby … but that could be at any time – the baby wasn't due for another six weeks. So, I sleep, boy, do I sleep. I was so far gone down the sleepy valley that our fine neighbour George, having called me on the phone several times (which, by the way, was beside me) resorted to throwing stones at our bedroom window to try and wake me. I'll explain why in a minute. I remember, somewhere in my dream, hearing the sound of the stones on the window, and thinking that it was just that – a dream. And then I woke up with a start, well actually more of a stop, then a start. George told me that my mother- and father-in-law had been ringing me to no avail, to tell me that Maria was heading down to theatre at the Coombe, long before her due date. Her high blood pressure meant that the baby would need to be delivered early.

I really don't know how I got from Portmarnock to the Coombe Hospital, but I did. It was almost teatime and I drove like a lunatic to get there and be with Maria. There must be 25 sets of lights between our house and the hospital, but I did the journey in 17 minutes, clearly not observing the rules even back then. I arrived just in time to see Maria making her way to the theatre to have a Caesarean section. Our baby was on her way and arriving early, very early. Six weeks early, in fact. I hadn't even hoovered in readiness for her arrival. What would she think? Well, I needn't have worried because she wouldn't be home for another three weeks. Dr Stewart at the Coombe Hospital was brilliant, chatting to me seemingly aimlessly and waiting for the moment when he would be called in to theatre. To me, this conversation all seemed to be in slow motion, as he asked me about holiday plans and other general chat, then he got the signal from the door and he was gone like Ronnie Delaney (for younger readers, this is the man who won gold in the 1500 metres at the 1956 Olympics in Melbourne), and I was left in the silence of the corridor, waiting. Maria had a whole team around her so I felt that she was in the best of hands, and then, after a short while, one of the nurses let me know I had a daughter. It was another 15 minutes before I saw her in her incubator with a little woolly hat on (on her, not on me) and instantly fell in love with her. From that moment on I knew everything had altered utterly and yet this strange feeling came over me, not of fear or trepidation but a sense of total, all-consuming love; a heartbeat that accelerated at a rate of knots.

She was absolutely tiny and weighed in at 3 lb 15 oz, the equivalent of two bags of sugar, and the biggest part of her was her beautiful brown eyes, but she was a fighter and has since proved to be strong as an ox. For years, people could never understand why I wouldn't eat lamb and the reason was because our baby looked like a lamb and I simply hadn't the heart. I realised this when I was driving down the country to a gig somewhere and noticed the lambs in the field, and they reminded me of Jessica. That was me cured of lamb on my plate for ever and a day.

Maria stayed in hospital for two weeks and, even when she got out, we still found ourselves in and out of the Coombe, feeding baby Jessica and willing her to get strong enough to come home. Maria remembers still how difficult it was to leave our tiny baby behind in hospital every night. Well, when she reached 5 lb in weight, she did come home and has been a joy ever since.

The adjustment at home was truly revolutionary. We had to get in gear pretty quickly, realising that this wasn't a rehearsal for anything, it was the real thing. And then there were all the accoutrements that go with having a baby in the house: the room done up for baby and the bottles, and the nappies, and the clothes – little clothes everywhere! Back in 1990, it was hard to find clothes to fit a premature baby, as I recall. But the one thing nobody prepares you for is the endless walking around the room or the landing while you try to get the wind out of a little baby. I found sitting down on a couch in the front room playing a particular song by Dan Fogelberg called 'Anastasia's Eyes' on the stereo and rubbing Jessica's back worked. See, getting her into music early. The lyrics are very strong and the words, about finding salvation in love of another, spoke to me, quite clearly. But you don't mind all this lack of sleep and general air of tiredness as a dad, because having a newborn in the house is so special. And, let's be honest, I didn't have the baby, so what had I got to complain about, I thought. I was just glad to be able to help out. Actually, I have that song playing as I write this and I'm right back there. Meantime, my daughter is across the room from me, immersed in her 20-something world. Should I remind her to burp?

Now we were this little family and the adjustments just got made; even if when we left home to go visit family or friends, we'd pack away so much stuff in the car that the neighbours thought we were leaving the country, and when we got home, it took about an hour to get everything into the house. But Jessica brought great love to us and she changed our lives for the better.

We had been married for five years before she arrived and had been happy out; working at our careers (Maria was still flying with Aer Lingus) and generally going about our lives like everyone else, but when Jessica arrived, we felt complete. Three years later, that feeling of completeness would be cemented with the arrival of Thomas in July 1993. I don't know why but I just assumed that Jessica would have a sister; odd, that. But when Thomas arrived, called after Maria's dad, who had passed away in March of that year, I was so filled with delight, and this time I was able to witness his arrival, which made it all the more special. The unconditional love came naturally with him as well. Here we were, a family of four, and Maria and I couldn't have been happier.

Now there is a certain innocence in being happy sometimes. For example, there really is quite a difference between having a girl in the house and a boy. Oh, yes. Of course, initially it makes no difference, but as time passes you begin to realise that there are fundamental differences between the two. Jessica was always a tidy eater, but with Thomas, we noticed that food didn't necessarily go from the spoon into his mouth automatically, oh no. Food could leave the spoon and land almost anywhere, like the bib or the table, of course, or the wall. And the wriggling when he didn't want to eat, sure you'd be worn out. He was his own man from the beginning and that's a good thing. From the moment Thomas arrived, Jessica decided he was hers to mind and became his second mother. I've no doubt Thomas has benefited from this all his life. In fact, the relationship between the two of them started so well and has progressed to the point that no one can come between them. They are truly made from the same cloth, each concerned with the welfare of the other.

They used to play a lot together as children. Jessica used to persuade Thomas to play with her Barbies, until Thomas would have enough and go off to find his cars. But she could always coax him back. They have a bond that even the great James would envy. I suppose it's natural anyway with siblings. They are both very self-possessed individuals with their own ideas on life and their own sense of who they are in the world. The wonderful thing is they both possess great heart and are now caring, warm and perfectly rounded adults (slim but perfectly rounded!)*

For us it was a huge change to have two children, but for my parents, it was a huge joy. They absolutely adored the children and would babysit at the drop of a hat. Before Thomas arrived, Jessica would be down with my folks as often as we'd let her and then, with Thomas, their joy was doubled, even if all my mother's good crockery was put away, and with good reason. It's incredible to watch a small boy as his hands constantly reach out for anything that might take his fancy. Nothing is too high, too low or too awkward to grasp at and that was Thomas, for years. But my parents were the ideal grandparents, who played games with them, like taking the kitchen furniture into the garden and pretending to be on the bus to Bray (a trip that was done in reality too). All of this, plus teaching them about the garden, taking them on day trips and outings to the theatre. For my parents, our two children were the only grandchildren they would have and they invested all their

---

✳ That reminds me of the story of the dad reading a Bible story to his young son. 'The man named Lot was warned to take his wife and flee out of the city, but his wife looked back and was turned into a pillar of salt.' His son said to him, 'Okay, but what happened to the flea?'

love in them. One of my favourite photos is one of my dad, Thomas and me at the end of lunch in our house one Father's Day, all smiling contentedly and happy in each other's company. That's why photographs are important: the ones you take on your phone can be lost or forgotten about. But the photographs you take with a camera you get developed, then frame that moment and feel the memory as if it was yesterday.

When my dad died, Jessica was eight and Thomas five, and there's no doubt their nanny became super important to them, and they to her, from this time on. Three best friends is what they developed into and continued until she died.

When you have children you quickly realise that they are individuals and that comparing one to the other is ridiculous. Yet we do it, not out of any malice, even if we shouldn't. With Jessica there seemed to be always a sense of order and relative quiet about the house, but with Thomas there seemed to be always a sense of disorder and absolutely no quiet about the house. I remember he went missing one day, could not be found anywhere. Panic ensued and a search continued high and low until he was eventually found in his friend Andre's house next door. They were best friends and would come and go always into each other's houses, but this particular morning Andre had gone out with his dad and nobody was home. Thomas let himself in via the open patio door and decided to hide behind the couch and wait for Andre to surprise him. Great idea, except he fell asleep on his teddy and thus

sica's
nunion.

The car thing
continues with
my son Thomas.

Neven – the reason my
taste buds are heightened.
(© *RTÉ Stills Library*)

Our family
NOT outside
our house.

Held up by the Roses.
(© *Irish Times*)

Van at Rose of Tralee.

Me off camera watching Van, thinking of my dad who died days earlier.

In Tralee – Noel Smyth, executive producer, and Dave Donaghy, director of the Rose of Tralee.

With the late author Pete McCarthy.

Legendary producer and friend Bil Keating.

With Tony Bennett.

The night Van launched his book at the Olympia. (© *John Minihan*)

With Sal Scognamillo and his dad at Patsy's, New York.

Put through my paces by Riverdance legends –
Celebrity Jigs and Reels judges Jean Butler and
Colin Dunne. (© *RTÉ Stills Library*)

Fun

Childhood hero, the late Val Doonican.

...rised at my 50th ...Howth by Maria ...nd the children.

Marty's Surprise Party!

The Maestro – Ennio Morricone gets to meet my family.

At Barack Obama's inauguration – early start.

Inauguration Ceremonies

JANUARY 20, 2009

ADMIT BEARER TO WEST FRONT OF CAPITOL

Gates open—9:00 A.M.
Musical Prelude—10:30 A.M.
Ceremonies—11:30 A.M.

Dianne Feinstein
Chairman,
Congressional Inaugural Committee

Ticket Holders will be required to
pass through security screening.
Please arrive early due to large crowds.

THIS TICKET DOES NOT ADMIT
TO CAPITOL BUILDING

WEST STANDING • PURPLE

ENTER PURPLE GATE

**Disco night at Squar̶
Lake, New England, U̶**

w York at Christmas.

Dr Gerald Keen delighted to congratulate me on winning *Celebrity Bainisteoir*. (© *Collins Photo Agency*)

Renée Fleming, Queen of the Metropolitan Opera.

My movie hero, Al Pacino.

Maria and me in the US, still holding hands.

My Eurovision and 2fm friend Larry Gogan.

My beautiful family, Christmas 2014. (© *Naomi Gaffey*)

Hair again. (© *RTÉ Stills Library*)

Winning Streak co-host and pal Sinéad Kennedy.

With Graham Norton, Eurovision 2015.

With Dr Peter Urban, German TV Eurovision commentator – a great Euro friend and a gentleman.

ORF
BUILDING BRIDGES
EuroVision
SONG CONTEST

D2

MARTIN
WHELAN

COMMENTATOR

RTÉ
IRELAND

EUROVISION

With John Kennedy O'Connor and Paul Clarke at Eurovision 2015.

With Buddy Collie, our faithful friend fifteen years, who went to Doggie Heaven at summer's end in 2015. (© *Brendan Burke, shootmydog.ie*)

Writing/speaking the book.

ensued a major SOS and panic on everyone's part. Jessica was so distressed, I think it's fair to say it would be another 10 years before she would let him out of her sight.

One of the lovely things for me is that they played happily together for much of their shared childhood and yet developed as true individuals. With Jessica, this meant Billy Barry for dancing and then ballet classes; for Thomas, the Billy Barry experience lasted one month – fair enough – however, his football began with the Nippers in Malahide United and continued for another 12 years. The amount of mucky fields and wind-swept side lines I have endured on Saturday or Sunday mornings, I'll never forget. I discovered streets I never heard of and will never see again, all in the cause of developing Tom's footballing prowess. He was good and loved it: took after his pops, Tom, Maria's Dad. Meanwhile, Jessica pursued her ballet right through into her early twenties, and she, too, was good and loved it. So they both found things they loved and excelled at them. Thomas and I still try to get to one match a year at Old Trafford because we love Manchester United and it's a real thrill for both of us to spend time together watching our favourite team. With Jessica we have attended lots of ballets over the years and her love for the dance remains undiminished.

We have also got enormous pleasure out of seeing Jessica and Thomas follow in their old dad's footsteps as altar servers, at our local church, St Nicholas of Myra in Kinsealy. They had the most wonderful priest there, Father Frank

Hyland. The man was a tonic and would give sermons that suggested a particularly Christian outlook on various topics and you just warmed to him. He was also lovely company. We all took part in the Masses at St Nicholas's, Jessica as altar server, Thomas as a collector and myself as a reader from time to time.

One Sunday Jessica was serving away, and when Mass had ended, Maria noticed the tabernacle was still open and gave Thomas the instruction to go back into the priest in the sacristy and tell him that the chalice was outside the tabernacle. Thomas completely forgot the words he needed to use and told Father Frank, and I quote, 'My mum says you need to put the cups in the press'. Out of the mouths of babes. The lapse on Father Frank's part was, I suppose, a sign of the beginnings of dotage. I liked him very much and enjoyed our chats, just like I did with many of the priests I knew when I was an altar boy: Father Mulvey, Father Martin, Father Casey, good men all. Or the vast majority of the Vincentians at St Paul's College: Father Keogh, our French master, referred to as Père Plum, which seems to me a perfect description of a small French teaching priest. Then there was father Joe McCann, a fine English teacher and responsible for Sing Out! and Father Jack Harris, one of my favourites, the priest who married myself and Maria and who christened Jessica and Thomas. A man who understood radio, motorbikes, chemistry, technology … a bright spark.

Over the years, my involvement with the Church has almost always been positive, which is why I have felt so happy about Jessica and Thomas being a part of it. I would have fundamental differences with the Church about gay relationships, married priests – just how bad would it be for a priest to be married with children and therefore fully understand what so many people go through in everyday life? – yet I am also a great respecter of the sacrifice that priests and nuns have made with their lives; their vocation has called them to give up so much.

The funny thing is, when you talk to nuns and priests about their faith, they don't talk about 'giving up', but instead about what they've gained. Which brings me to faith. Not theirs; mine.

I wouldn't consider myself a good Catholic. I do the best I can, but fall a lot; however, I'd like to think I'm a half-decent Christian. I try to do a bit of good and not to cause too much bother. I would never knowingly set out to hurt anybody and, in spite of all the trials and tribulations of life, I have never lost faith in God.* It's impossible to try and explain to anybody with even a smidgen of cynicism how it is that a grown adult has a strong faith based on nothing but what he was taught in school and is carrying that with him through life. But that's me. My parents were great believers, too, and they instilled in me a faith that I've kept

---

✻ Which reminds me of the fellow with the placard walking up and down the main street. Written on it is, 'Jesus is coming. Look busy.' And here's another one: Do you know what's making a comeback? Reincarnation.

with me ever since and that I've passed on in turn to my own children. It's all based on blind faith and no one can prove any of it right or wrong. All the conversations over dinner and theological seminars coming out of your ears neither prove nor disprove anything. So the belief stays and, quite frankly, I feel better for it. It's good for my head to believe in another place and that all of this life has some point to it. I can't accept that this is all there is and that when we die it's over. I want to believe that when I pass over (die, there it is, I've put it down) I will find myself in another world. I want to meet my mum and dad again and possibly Frank Sinatra, Spencer Tracy, Margaret Rutherford and Alastair Sim. I want to imagine my Auntie Kay in a shimmering frock dancing with Matt Monro to 'My Kind of Girl', or my Auntie Evelyn, who worked for RTÉ in the early days, having dinner with Eamonn Andrews, or, one of my favourite imaginings, my Uncle Michael the Christian Brother married with three children and comparing sacred arias with Pavarotti. Mad or what, and yet, why not? Why shouldn't I imagine that heaven will involve the joy of being in the presence of our Lord Jesus Christ, but also some very fine restaurants, wine of the consistent quality of an Amarone, a balmy climate and the opportunity to be in the presence of those you've loved and lost? If I can believe that, then that's good enough for me and, of course, with that belief goes the understanding that those who follow me will find me and want to spend time with me. Look at the reams of books on shelves all over the world on faith, on religion, on belief. Listen to the work of Van Morrison and his search for a belief structure, which has caused him to write some of the most beautiful songs ever written: 'Across the Bridge Where Angels Dwell', or 'Enlightenment', or 'A Sense of Wonder', or 'In the Garden'. Have a listen to them and you'll know what I mean. It's good to have a little faith, it helps you through when things are not so good, and if you let it sit lightly on your shoulders when things are going your way, it's a comfort. Because no matter how jolly you are, how well you think you are or how well you have adjusted to this world, it's good to have something to cling to in rough seas. And remember the tune that's going to play when I'm leaving the church, the swelling orchestral notes of 'Deborah's Theme' by Ennio Morricone, from the film *Once Upon a Time in America*.

...

But all this has taken me away from the children for a bit. Val Doonican's song 'The Special Years' was a hit for him in 1965 and the lyrics read as true today as they did 50 years ago: 'From pigtails to wedding veils, from pinafores to lace, and in between are the special years time never can erase. From play toys to college boys, from little girl to wife, and in between are the special years you remember all of your life.' It ends with the line: 'Just stay awhile in the special years. Their magic will soon be gone.' It's so true that the special years are years to cherish. They can't last for ever, of course, and yet we've never wanted our children to be any older than they were and also never wished for them to fly the nest. We have always loved having them about and to this day they remain with us. Is there to be no escape?

Along the way, there's the pleasure of holidays taken, drives to school listening to Adele or Counting Crows or Paul Simon and his song about a father and daughter; going with Thomas to see Deep Purple play at The Point and him falling asleep (which, considering the decibel level of Deep Purple, is a feat that probably ranks in the *Guinness Book of Records*). Jessica and I stood in front of the stage when Adele played at the Olympia and loved every minute of it, and then there was the excitement of the arrival of the new James Bond film, Thomas meeting Pierce Brosnan and being thrilled, but Maria, my current wife, seemed far more thrilled! All these things stay with you. I remember the time we went skiing together and Maria and I spent the entire week on our bums because we couldn't stand on the skis, let alone go anywhere; meanwhile, the children were on the black slopes in almost no time.

When both of them were born, I remember the feeling, as does Maria, of being in love with the children, not just loving them. Nowadays, they are constantly on my mind, no matter where I am or what I'm doing. The exotica of Azerbaijan for the Eurovision Song Contest, presenting *Winning Streak* on the television, playing music and having the craic on Lyric FM with *Marty in the Morning,* or judging some event for charity in a hall in the middle of Ireland. There's always a call from one of them about something, even something trivial. But I love that. This quartet is as close as close can be: the four musketeers, one for all and all for one. Proof of this must be the fact that we have had a family holiday every year; it remains one of the great joys of my life to spend time with the three people I love most in the world. We're just delighted that they still want to come away with us and those holidays in sun-kissed locations linger on in the memory and can give you a warm glow on a rainy November afternoon back home. Maria's mum came with us a few times on summer holidays – fortunately I loved my mother-in-law (no, seriously, I did). Not for me the Les Dawson routine: 'The only success the mother-in-law ever had was with the council, selling her mince pie lids as manhole covers', or, 'I took my mother-in-law to Madame Tussaud's Chamber of Horrors and one of the attendants said, "Keep her moving, Sir, we are stocktaking".' Seriously, it was a pleasure to have her along on some of our Canary Island trips. Sadly, as you know, my parents wouldn't fly, and rowing from Dublin to Torremolinos would take ages! Anyway, my father didn't have the arms for it.

We also had some lovely holidays in Malta, and I remember our first holiday in particular, just outside Valetta. We enrolled soccer-mad Thomas in the Gary Neville football summer school, and I was there in a minding capacity (well, I was hardly there in a playing capacity). I joined a group of sports journalists who were interviewing Gary Neville by the side of the pitch. It was fun and he proved to be an illuminating interviewee, even if neither of us had a clue what the other was talking about. I also fondly remember Thomas and Jessica hiding from the kids' club organiser by diving into the swimming pool ... not a fool-proof plan. However, one of the best trips we ever had as a family was a celebration of our 25th wedding anniversary. I know, you're probably thinking, why wouldn't they go off, the two of them? But that's just us.

Off we went to America and covered Santa Barbara, San Francisco and Las Vegas. We simply had the best time and all of us found things of interest on the trip. It was a sight to behold as Maria and Jessica decided to go for a shop on Rodeo Drive and for reasons I cannot explain, my credit card disappeared, vanished like a trick by David Copperfield, amazing. Unusually on this trip I had a day out by myself. Maria and the children decided to check out Muscle Beach in Santa Monica and all the beautiful people. I didn't want to overshadow anybody, so I kept away. Instead I took myself off and drove along Santa Monica Freeway onto Santa Ana Freeway, ending up about half an hour later at Yorba Linda Boulevard. I pulled up at number 18001, the home of the Richard Nixon Library & Birthplace. I just immersed myself in it for most of the day. Nixon has been a passion of mine (I may have mentioned this before), so to be in this place was something I'll never forget. Obviously I had to get a replica tie pin, the old campaign badges and yet another book. I sat and thought, I stood by the graveside and prayed, and afterwards I drove back to the gang. To their credit, they wanted to know everything, or at least pretended to want to know everything.

We moved on to San Francisco along Highway One, our dreams of driving along Big Sur becoming a reality, and then there was our final stop, Las Vegas. We had never been and knew it only through reading about it, as well as from watching Elvis and Sinatra and movies like *Casino* and *Oceans 11, 12* and *13*. It's madder than you think. The heat is unbelievable (you're in the desert, for heaven's sake), the hotels are the size of small towns and everyone is out to make a buck.

Two problems arose when we were there. First, Thomas was only 17 at the time and therefore couldn't go near any of the gambling tables or even the machines. (We don't gamble, so it didn't matter to us, but by the same token, what were we doing in Vegas?) I suppose the great comedian Rodney Dangerfield puts it very plainly: 'How do you leave Las Vegas with a small fortune? Go in with a big one.' Second, at 20, Jessica couldn't enjoy a glass of wine legally there, so we became members of the criminal fraternity fairly quickly. But we all loved it with its great expanse and everything being over the top.

Two memories of our trip to Vegas will stay with me all my days and both are down to Maria. She's a great one for the added value on a trip. I'll come up with the idea and plan it, but she always sees other possibilities. So, thanks to her, we had a hot air balloon ride at dawn over Vegas – awesome – and the other was a helicopter ride over the Grand Canyon, which I found terrifying and exciting. Quite frankly, I must have lost half a gallon of perspiration with the nerves. It didn't help that, as he flew over, our pilot played the 'Ride of the Valkyries'.

We touched down at an outpost and played at being cowboys for a couple of hours before flying back. I liked being a cowboy, walking round in chaps and speaking in a kind of drawl while hearing strains of *The Virginian* and *Bonanza* or, indeed, *The High Chapparal*, in my head and then, as cowboys do, having an oul spit and it dribbling down the front of your shirt! Not a good look at all for a manly man.

Which reminds me of a funny story. Later that day we were walking around Las Vegas, and at every turn somebody was selling bottled water. It was Thomas who noticed that the man selling water was our helicopter pilot. Mad, but true ... and slightly worrying. So he was flying helicopters over the Grand Canyon at dawn and then selling dollar bottles of water from a cooler box on the street in the afternoon. In America, a dollar is a dollar.*

Before I forget, if you find yourself making the trip from Santa Monica to San Francisco, you have to call and see the Madonna Inn Resort and Spa on Highway 101 south of San Luis Obispo. It's the Old West-meets-Hawaii-meets-Spanish architecture, a mixture of bungalows and a fairy palace, with buildings of every colour imaginable and an interior filled with colour and daftness. It's the maddest place I've ever seen, like something dreamt up by Tim Burton having been fed blue Smarties by Johnny Depp for an hour. It's gorgeous and crazy all in one and I don't think

 And here's a cowboy question: 'What did the cowboy say when his dog left?' Answer: 'Doggone'. Oh, well.

there's anywhere else like it in the world. Years later, all we have to do is say, 'Madonna Inn', and we all know what we're on about. That's part and parcel of the four of us sharing these holidays: shared memories and warm ones at that. Priceless.

...

As I sit here sharing these memories with you, I realise how much we've shared as a family, all through our lives. But, of course, it's not all just about the big holidays. It's not always even about the big exam or being let down by a boyfriend or girlfriend or some huge trauma that's befallen them: more often than not it's the little things, the everyday things. Sharing a home is one thing, but sharing a life is something else. It's things like asking the question, 'How was your day?' and listening to the answer and enjoying the conversation that follows. Thank God we have that in our house. Being there when your children need you is so important. Now, not every day is a bed of roses, nor could it be, because life gets in the way and we all have to deal with and adapt to circumstances as we find them. But if you have issues or problems and you keep them bottled up inside, then they become more difficult to deal with. So when any of us finds ourselves with stuff going on, we talk about it and we all rally round to make things right. That's family. That's where I come from with my parents and it's how we operate in our home. We are glass-half-full kind of people. I find that sometimes it's just about asking the question, letting it sit and then waiting for the conversation to happen. Given time, it does.

We've shared so much over the years that at this stage, though we are always going to be their parents and they are always going to be our children, we're friends. That's what you would always hope your children would become. Friends with benefits, I'll grant you; benefits like food, drink, lodgings, heat, holidays, a well-stocked fridge and on and on. Now, the four of us get to go out and share special moments together like Ennio Morricone's visit to the 3 Arena with his 100-piece orchestra and 100-person choir … heavenly. At the Morricone concert I had a strange moment of flashback. I never actually told any of the family this, but as his music transported me, I suddenly remembered a trip we made many years ago to visit Santa in Rovaniemi in Lapland. It was one of the most magical things I've ever experienced. The twinkling lights, elves at your elbow, the snow, the forest and the big man himself, Santa. I remember it as clearly as if it were yesterday. Santa came to visit all of us in a wooden house set in the woods, I remember, and there was so much excitement in the air. The children were so high with expectation that even the parents began to get quite thrilled at the notion that Santa would soon be here. Well, he arrived out of the darkness on his sleigh pulled by a couple of reindeer and proceeded to chat with each of the children, dispensing gifts and being all you'd hoped he'd be. After some time he left, just as he had arrived, and disappeared into the darkness, waving back at our assembled group of gawping adults and elated children. Our two were beside themselves with happiness and I'll never forget their little faces on that night. I turned to Maria and said to her that we had truly met Santa, that's just how it felt.

The music at the concert had no link whatsoever with Lapland and yet I suppose it might have been just a feeling. Here I was, with the people I wanted to be with most in the world, being taken back to another special time.

Now, while I remember, some genius on the Lapland trip suggested that the children would really enjoy a trip on a snowmobile with Daddy driving and Mammy in a navigating capacity. Basically I drove this scooter affair with the children in a kind of bucket being pulled behind us through snow-laden forests at considerable speed. We whooshed off with the rest of them and were thrilled to hear the peals of laughter from the children as we sped on, 007 style. It all went on for a bit and we could hear the yelps of our children, clearly having a great time. When we eventually halted and walked back to the children the reason for the yelping became evident. Thomas has lost his gloves and his tiny little hands were freezing, almost frostbitten, and Jessica had been trying to tell us. I'm not convinced he's forgiven me for this. Oh, well. We also took to riding, or should that be sliding, on a toboggan. In true Marty fashion, they all slid along on their toboggan, while I fell off mine!*

 Which reminds me: What do you get from sitting on the snow for too long? Polaroids.

Discussions around the table these days are healthy and wide ranging, now that the children are adults. Jessica is embarking on a career in teaching, while Thomas has opted for marketing/event management. They still have time to sit and chat with their folks. We love being together and because they have seen the ups and downs of my business, they've also witnessed the highs and lows of family life. One big thing we have also done as a family is to build our own home, which we did with the help of architects Liam Tuite and Fran Whelan and a 'can-do, that's-no-problem' builder called Donogh Higgins. They were so great to work with and encouraged us all the way. To get the chance to design and build a house to your specifications and desires, to end up with the home of your dreams, is a real privilege. With all these people on board to make our vision come true, and Maria's innate sense of interior design, we created an oasis of calm and we love coming home. It's a great house for parties, large and small, and many's the night we have broken bread and supped fine wine with our family and friends. We have created a 'lovely home' for ourselves and for our children.

If there's any lesson to be learned from having children it's this: raise them as best you can, love and nourish them and, in time, become friends. Share your world with them, including all the ups and downs (not to the extent that you might scare them, by the way), and as you head in to your potential dotage you'll have children who will want to share their thoughts, hopes, dreams and aspirations with you. These days, when my son or daughter sits down beside us and produces the phone to show us some message or photograph or to share some mad news story from the other side of the world, I feel good, because they want to share their lives with us. They are our friends and we theirs.

I hope we'll hang about long enough to take their children to the zoo, if they're lucky enough to have them, and to look after them, like my parents looked after Jessica and Thomas. But I suppose what we both want is for them to find someone to be with, someone who will care for them the way we care for each other. As Ella Fitzgerald sang, 'Someone to Watch over Me'. You can't live other people's lives for them, but you can steer and hope and be there. If there's one thing I've learned from being a dad, it's that everything is a phase, I suppose: there's the sporting field and wondering if they'll get picked; there are the exams, the Junior and Leaving Certs and what they determine in terms of the future; there's college, and we worry about what course they've chosen and if they'll survive it and stay the course; then there's the hunt for work, and the small matter of a social life. You hope and pray that they'll find happiness, whatever they comprehend that to be. Because when we are gone and they carry on, which is the natural order, our fervent wish is for there to be someone to stand beside them to hold hands with, and for them to look out for each other.

Our unconditional love continues for as long as we do, Jessica and Thomas. We love you. As John Martyn said, 'May you never lay your head down without a hand to hold. May you never make your bed out in the cold.'

'What's Another Year'/'Hold Me Now'

Johnny Logan

When our driver, Majid, collected us from Flughafen Wien-Schwechat – that's Vienna International Airport to the likes of you and me – and drove us the 11 miles to central Vienna for Eurovision 2015, I wondered why I'd never made a trip here before. It's a beautiful city and only steeped in culture and, by all accounts, the location of the very first roll ... the Vienna roll!

As we drove along from the outskirts into the city proper, I began to reflect on all the Eurovision Song Contests I have known. Each time you arrive in the host city, you find billboard posters all over the place in recognition of the fact that you are at the heart of that year's Eurovision. You are met at the airport by volunteers who meet and greet all the delegates and organise your transport to your hotel and generally ensure that you have some sense of your surroundings as you acclimatise to a week in the Eurovision bubble. Because a bubble it is. For most delegations, it's two weeks in which the act representing the country becomes immersed in the event, and prior to the first semifinal, truth be told, everybody believes they can win the thing. The fact is, they become stars for the duration of their stay and there are camera crews and journalists hanging on their every word until ... they don't win and they return to the love of their own people. This event has a lot to do with national pride and having won it more than anyone else (seven times, in case you're counting), we are particularly proud of having boxed above our weight. Because we've succeeded, as a tiny nation, in achieving so many victories, we always attend with a real air of positivity and a belief that we can win it again. If it weren't for the Swedes we might actually have a chance; damn ABBA and their H_2O toilet song, which changed the game for the contest.

...

My first encounter with the Eurovision Song Contest dates back to 1965, when I was a very small boy sitting at home watching television with my mum and dad, launching into a large bar of Cadbury's Dairy Milk, pen in hand and the *RTÉ Guide* open at the Eurovision page so we could do the votes and then compare ours with those of the 18 countries taking part. We cheered loudly when the Irish entry that year, Butch Moore, sang 'Walking the Streets in the Rain' (for ever etched in my brain as 'Walking with Magritte and Lorraine', not sure why that is). We cheered even louder when Ireland came sixth. Coupled with Butch Moore's great performance was the fact that the show was coming to us live from Naples in Italy – exotic or what? The following year, it was the turn of Dickie Rock and 'Come Back to Stay', which made it to number four: top man, Dickie. So the event was part and parcel of our television year, like the Rose of Tralee, the *Late Late Show* and the Angelus.

As viewers we had been with this contest for well over 20 years when I got the opportunity to present the National Song Contest on the telly with Maxi in 1987 from the Gaiety Theatre in Dublin. There were nine acts in contention and Johnny Logan won, singing his own song, 'Hold Me Now', with a passion I knew he possessed but which, seen up close, was something else. He was the outright and absolute winner on the night, soaring away from his nearest rival, Paul Duffy.

And so I got the chance to compère my very first Eurovision Song Contest. I didn't know what to expect, except that the excitement I felt was like nothing I had ever experienced before. I found myself at the Palais du Centenaire in Brussels on 9 May 1987, in the company of producer Ian McGarry, looking forward to meeting up with Terry Wogan. As this was my first Eurovision, I needed to take her handy, I decided, nice and slow, get used to it and then eventually get up to speed. I had no chance this night: Johnny Logan took to the stage with the force of a tornado. He knew the difference it would make to a career that had faltered and needed this win so badly. It seemed to me that, apart from his brother Michael, Johnny seemed to be on his own. Well, he did it by a particularly good margin, beating Germany into second place (just like he had back in 1980 with Shay Healy's wonderful 'What's Another Year') and made Eurovision history, being the only artist to win the contest twice. He would go on to be the only person to win the event three times when he wrote 'Why Me?' for Linda Martin and she stole the show in Malmö in Sweden in 1992.

The thrill of being there in Brussels and commentating on Johnny's second win for Ireland was just fabulous. He came to the event as a Eurovision star anyway, but now he was practically out of the firmament. I have a memory of him climbing a step ladder to place a glass on a huge pyramid of champagne glasses and thinking to myself, He's gonna fall, but he didn't; he carried it off beautifully. (Incidentally, one of my favourite songs of all time remains the Italian entry from 1987, 'Gente di Mare'.)

So that was it. I was hooked. The daftness of the Eurovision had bitten me and I was unlikely ever to be able to shake it off. Of course, there are always going to be some peculiar moments at the Eurovision, and I can still remember, at my first contest, meeting Plastic Bertrand in the lift. He was, in fact, Roger Allen Jouret from Brussels and was representing Luxembourg with a song called

'Amour, Amour'. He came second last. He was not a happy bunny as he had clearly seen the Eurovision as a chance to revitalise his career, having had a Europe-wide hit in 1978 with 'Ça Plane Pour Moi'. The Plastic I met was not particularly communicative, but beautifully turned out in a purple jacket of the bolero variety, just like Johnny's on the night, in fact. My attempt at some sort of communication with the plastic one fell on deaf ears. (Which reminds me of the plastic surgeon, who, when asked if he had had any unusual requests from patients, replied, 'I've raised a few eyebrows'.)

Maxi and I presented the National Song Contest the following year at the Olympia Theatre, when 'Jump the Gun' won the chance to represent Ireland, in Ireland, as we were the hosts in 1988, thanks to Johnny. Then there was a hiatus while I made my spectacular leap into the unknown and left the warmth of Donnybrook behind for a couple of years (as outlined earlier) and closed off my links to the Eurovision Song Contest for some years to come. But we always watched it, and when I returned to RTÉ, I hoped that I might get the chance to be involved again. The opportunity arose in 2000 when Pat Kenny moved to a Saturday evening TV slot and I was offered the job of compère. I hesitated for about eight seconds and then took on the task. Roll on Stockholm in Sweden.

For you history-lovers, the concept of the Eurovision Song Contest is based on a competition at the San Remo music festival in Italy in the fifties. The festival's idea was that each

participating country was to enter a song that would be performed live on TV and radio (simultaneously and at the
same time) and all the countries would then vote for their
favourite. Europe in the mid-fifties was rebuilding itself
after World War Two and this was seen as a way of bringing
all of the continent together in a light-entertainment
fashion, thus cementing the links between all these nations.
Technologically it required a leap of faith as satellite television did not even exist and so a system based on a terrestrial
microwave network was used. In the years since there have
been quite a few songs I'd like to microwave!

The original contest took place in Lugano in Switzerland
in 1956 and seven countries participated. To give you some
perspective on where it's gone since, in 2015, 27 countries
participated in the grand final. However, to get to that
number, 33 countries battled it out in two semi-finals for
20 places in the final. The other seven places were made
up of the big five; Germany, France, the United Kingdom,
Italy and Spain (the five countries that pay the most to the
European Broadcasting Union), as well as the previous
year's winner and the host nation. My God, I'm getting a
headache. Then, of course, Australia joined us as part of
the 60th year celebrations. There you go, Eurovision not
letting the small matter of geography get in the way of a
good story. Still, with a nod and a wink in the general
direction of world peace and harmony, bring it on. And
the Australian involvement was great fun anyway. (Not
that it did us any good, unfortunately, in 2015. That's the
problem in a contest that has so many contenders. Every

year, we set out, full of good heart and great expectations, to do our best, but every year, little Ireland has to fight its corner and get out of the semi-final.)

Meantime, back in Stockholm 2000 ... I found myself, 13 years on from my last Eurovision, at a quite different event. It was taking place in the Globe Arena, seating 16,000, the biggest audience to date, and everything seemed quite vast. I loved being back in the thick of it and the entry this year for Ireland by Eamonn Toal, 'Millennium of Love', did us proud, coming in at number six. But I knew that my love affair with the Eurovision Song Contest was cemented when Stefan Raab took to the stage for Germany, with backing singers dressed as cowboys in gold-and-white reflective suits. The song was 'Wadde Hadde Dudde Da'. Not to be outdone, the Swedes sent Roger Pontare dressed as a native American accompanied by a pow-wow dancer, a Norwegian Sami and an Eskimo singing about indigenous people fighting for their land. They even had a bit of fire going on stage for the purposes of a bit of heat.

I'm indebted to the San Marino commentator John Kennedy O'Connor and his book, *The Eurovision Song Contest: 50 Years,* for reminding me of the pleasures that reignited my fire at Eurovision in 2000. This was the year the Olsen Brothers, two older gentlemen, won it for Denmark with 'Fly on the Wings of Love', and I believe our head of delegation, Niamh, fell slightly in love with the pair of them. Having seen quite a number of these people over the years, there's precious little chance you'd be falling in love with them – sadly, they'd need to fall out of love with themselves first – but what is quite endearing about some of the loopier entrants is that they know this is all a bit of fun, and, from a television point of view, they are giving us really fabulous entertainment, even though some of them do need locking up. In the time I've been doing the show, we've had a man dressed in a tinfoil housecoat (Verka), Polish milkmaids, a veritable plethora of warriors of one kind or another, the six Russian grannies, gymnasts, knitters ... but, sure, we even had Jedward with 'Waterfall', and let's not even discuss Dustin. That all adds to the gaiety of the event, its glitz, its glamour and its fun. But fundamentally it really does come down to a good song, and almost always there are two or three really good songs, and they are the ones that vie for the top spot every year. I remember in particular the 2007 winner in Helsinki. It was called 'Molitva' and was sung by Marija Šerifoviç from Serbia. It was the first ballad to win since 1996 and there wasn't a word of English in it, but it was a straightforward hit song.

...

This event has taken me to places I might never have seen; Stockholm, Copenhagen, Tallinn, Riga, Istanbul, Kiev, Athens, Helsinki, Belgrade, Moscow, Oslo, Düsseldorf (well, I was there on an Aer Lingus overnight a few times), Baku, Malmö, Vienna, oh, yes, and Brussels back in '87. On every occasion there's been great excitement and whoever it was that was sent to represent Ireland always gave the best they could – after that, it was in the lap of the gods. I remember falling in love with Athens, which hosted the contest in 2004. I think it was something to do with the fact that there seemed to be sand in everything I ate and drank. The people were incredibly friendly and even back in 2004, I noticed that they had a particular fondness for you paying cash for your dinner. In fact, almost all the transactions I made seemed to involve cash and my little credit card was spurned at every opportunity. They were efficient, though. There was a tobacconist on the corner from our hotel and I noticed he had a Zippo lighter with Frank Sinatra's likeness on it. I had that one but there was another one that I wanted so I asked the guy if he could get hold of it. Off he went, returning with a brochure in his hand, pointing out the Zippo I wanted. I ordered it on the spot, returned three days later and he had it. Now that's service, efficient and with a smile. Oh, and cash will do nicely.

Every weekend there seemed to be a protest in the centre of Athens – there have been a fair few since – but they are part of the city's culture. I do also remember going shopping around the Acropolis for some souvenirs to take home as gifts: the shopkeepers kept handing me this ornament of some Greek mythological fellow with a huge willy who, at the press of a button, shouted 'Eurovision' at me. I feel they may have missed the essence of what the competition is about. I actually did contemplate bringing one of these lads home for my mother as a nod in the general direction of Greek mythology. At least she'd have somewhere to hang her dishcloth!

...

Now, while the competition might seem to be a madcap adventure, quite a lot of preparation goes into it. Every commentator has a pigeonhole, a slot where information from all the other countries is deposited for you to go over and include in your own commentary, if possible. Back in the day, there was so much paper used for this purpose, small forests must have been depleted for years. Deirdre Horlecker, my broadcast assistant, and I worked tirelessly, pasting and cutting up bits of paper and putting it all together for the big night. Technology has made it easier to do this now and we have a system that works very well. Gráinne Ní Fhlatharta works with me and has done for the past number of years. Just like Deirdre, she is super efficient and therefore it all goes like clockwork. See? You think I stroll in and am handed a stiff drink and a canapé or three and away I go: not so.

We arrive the weekend before the event and there are commentator meetings on Monday, Wednesday and Friday. We have to attend them because that's where all the information is shared about the event, venue, sound and lighting. We meet the other commentators, which is, for me, the real joy of the whole event. These are special people who, like me, have suffered for their art and battled on, knowing that there can be pain along the way, to bring the joy of Eurovision to our people back in the safety of their homes. Thank God, even with the difference in languages we all possess a similar sense of humour about the event. Like me, they take the event very seriously, but not themselves. So it's a fun get-together. There's the marvellous and bold

Dr Peter Urban providing the German commentary (always good for a bit of divilment at our meetings, a little bit of cat-among-the-pigeons stuff, like how come there is no loo on our gantry). Keeping the Swedes informed is Edward af Sillén, probably one of the most handsome men on the planet: you just stand beside him to make him look even better. He has the most perfect English and is always a pleasure to spend time with, funny with it, too. Our man in San Marino, well, their man, is John Kennedy O'Connor, writer of the aforementioned bible of the Eurovision, its official history. He is actually based in California, but loves the event with a passion (he tutored me when I ended up on Ken Bruce's BBC Radio 2 Eurovision quiz in 2014. I was up against Scott Mills, a Eurovision expert of sorts. Just the two of us and I just about scraped in second. Nice coaching, John. He is also the best of company.) Meantime, our friends in the Antipodes, Australia, send Julia Zemiro and Sam Pang with the lovely Paul, head of delegation; yet again there's fun to be had with them. I still miss one of the veterans of the event, Jean-Pierre Hautier, who gave the Walloons his all from 1994 until 2012 when he passed away. A tall and very distinguished man was Jean-Pierre, a gentleman of the old school. I particularly remember his company in 2005 in Kiev when the Orange Revolution had ushered in a new sense of freedom in Ukraine. We cheered them with a glass of whatever was handy and a passing cheroot!

Michael Kealy is our head of delegation for RTÉ at the song contest and does a great job. He has a quiet efficiency

about him and nothing is left to chance. He is a pleasure
as a travelling companion, an all-round good guy, and is
truly attentive to a commentator and his colleague high in
the rafters of an arena somewhere in Europe. We are a tiny
team and he makes it all the more pleasurable with his
unswerving affability. Also, I'd be lost without the incredible expertise of Paul G. Sheridan. This man eats, sleeps
and drinks the Eurovision Song Contest, and anything that
you need to know, he will know. He is a fact-checker extraordinaire. He also possesses an enormous Eurovision
record collection and whenever called upon, he will regale
the world with Eurovision. He is also a very good person
and an invaluable part of our little group. The thing about
Paul is he really gets the Eurovision and lets a lot of the
nonsense wash over him, while making sure that the business is attended to. Great guy. You are better off by far
having people like these in your life. They add greatly to
the gaiety of the nation and make the job at hand all the
more enjoyable. In fact, now that the Australians are to
take part on a regular basis, I must talk to Michael. They'd
probably want to stage it sometime if they won, no doubt
at Sydney Opera House. We could be away for weeks ...

One of the great joys of the Eurovision is the 'social
element', as my old school teacher used to say. A lunch in
Moscow with Larry Gogan and a light supper with Kevin
Lenihan in Copenhagen have been two of my delights
along the way. These are two of the finest men it's been
my privilege to know in the business. Larry is a legend for
all the right reasons and is a gorgeous companion over a

meal. I am so glad that nobody has ever recorded our conversations because libel wouldn't know where to look. We put the world to rights generally and have fun doing it. (Mind, at the gates of the Kremlin, I did attempt to sell him, but they were having none of it. Their loss.) Producer Kevin Lenihan has been a friend for years and a valued colleague. When I returned to RTÉ from my two years of peculiar carry on, he was a good and true friend and ally. From his production abilities to his work as head of delegation for Eurovision, as well as his work as head of variety in television, he is integrity personified. We have shared a love of Van Morrison and the Great American Songbook for over 20 years and we're also both partial to a small glass of red to wash down the bit of dinner. His unswerving belief that we can win Eurovision again has stayed with me.

Julian Vignoles and David Blake Knox, who have both been heads of delegation in their time, have also played a major part in this journey, and their belief in what we are trying to do also keeps the idea afloat. Lads, we will get there eventually. Both Julian and David have written very fine books on the Eurovision from an Irish perspective, *Inside the Eurovision* and *Ireland and the Eurovision* respectively, and if you really want to understand where we are and, just as important, where we've been, then pick them up and make two very decent lads a few bob.

One other little nugget about the competition: while you're at home enjoying the spectacle and I'm trying to make sense of it on your behalf, I like to share a glass of Bailey's during the voting section. Sometimes it seems the voting lasts just as long as the actual event, so a little drink helps. It was back in 1987 that Terry Wogan, the legendary BBC Eurovision commentator, sent me down a glass of Bailey's by way of welcome. I never forgot it, nor indeed the bottle of Bailey's, when we would make our way in to our commentary booth at the top of the arena. From Sweden through Turkey and on to Austria that creamy taste of Ireland has accompanied our voting segment. Ivor Lyttle, who takes charge of all the commentators' needs (he has a proper job with a nautical hue back home in Germany), has minded us well in this regard, too, and ensured a plentiful supply of ice for the weary broadcaster. So thank you, Terry, for an idea that we continue to honour. Some day, somewhere, we will raise a glass in celebration of yet another Irish win at the Eurovision Song Contest. After all, the only thing we need would be votes.

...

Speaking of votes, I found myself at the helm of the auspicious televisual delight that is the Rose of Tralee back in 1997 and, looking back, I don't suppose I knew what hit me. I took over from the late, lamented Derek Davies and I suppose I went for it in a real sense. Obviously I was thrilled when I was offered it and felt I could put my own stamp on it.

The whole idea of it is completely and utterly daft on paper. Let's see, we'll put on a live TV show from a tent in a car park around the last week in August, when people are out trying to get the last of the summer sunshine and we'll put it on on a Monday and Tuesday night. And we'll search for a girl to represent all that is good in our Irishness. It's not a talent contest nor a beauty contest nor a brains contest nor a … well, you get the picture. It's none of these and all of these. It's trying to please three sorts of people, the TV audience, the dome audience and the girls themselves.

The first thing you must do with the Rose of Tralee is leave your cynical hat outside. You are now entering a very different world and you need to be able to let yourself go in it. Because the very essence of this event is a celebration of our Irishness, and the fact that people who live away from Ireland are somewhat more Irish than we are is neither here nor there. But in fact it's more there than here … oh, no, here comes the headache again.

In case you aren't familiar with this fabulous event, it begins with a ball on the Friday night where everyone is introduced on stage to the audience and the TV masses (the Roses have been here for 10 days already) and the festivities begin. On Saturday and Sunday, the producer, researcher and I interview each of the girls. It's all very light-hearted and chatty, just like the event on the night, except it is important to try and get at least one different moment from each of the girls because, after all, it is a television entertainment and you want it to be as good as it can be. The show runs over two nights, and on the

Tuesday night, the excitement is like that of an All-Ireland final. It's going out live on RTÉ, on t'internet and on the RTÉ player, with about three-quarters of a million viewers watching each night. No bother. When I presented the show, Noel Smyth was at the helm as executive producer and Dave Donaghy directed: I felt in safe hands.

As for the Roses, well, they have turned up on the night to do the best they can and they'd rarely let you down. But, don't forget, we are dealing with about 16 Roses each night and it must be really daunting for them. Never mind that they've gone to university, where they aren't sure whether it's going to be rocket science or law, with a bit of medicine thrown in for good measure: the moment each girl arrives on stage, all that goes out the window. There's a huge welcome, with roars and screams from strangers, but that's the Irish way. The girl walks up to stand beside the presenter at the microphone, the famous two-pronged microphone, and away we go. I can only imagine how nerve-racking that is, in spite of all the practice the girls do. The moment has arrived. The entire family have made the trip from Milwaukee or wherever, all the relations in Ireland are out and you have three minutes to impress the judges. Meantime, downstage, the scrubbed and smiling faces of the Garda band are beaming up at the stage, the arc lighting bouncing off the shiniest of heads! Here we go. Showtime.

During my time as presenter, I only remember one 'disaster', if you can call it that. One of the Roses came up on stage and I asked a question and got nothing in response.

I asked a second and a third – nothing. Absolute silence. There is a moment in an entertainment programme, particularly a live one, where you know things aren't going well. She started to shake, I took her hand to calm her, and then we were both shaking. I was wearing an earpiece, which you do so that help can come in the form of a different question or a prompt to help the situation. I waited another moment and asked another question as she just dried up completely. She was like a rabbit in the headlights. At this point, Dave Donaghy came on the earpiece and said, 'You're on your own, kid,' and started to laugh. I've never quite forgiven him. Somewhere inside, I started to laugh, too, but outwardly kept up the bit of decorum. We didn't detain her for a party piece; it seemed pointless.

I think in all the time I presented the Rose of Tralee this was the only problematic entrant I had to deal with and I really felt for her. Yes, nerves and butterflies are a good thing because they make you perform better, but these are not professional performers; these are girls from Ireland and right across the world, who have grown up with a belief in themselves, in Ireland, in the joy of achievement, and with a very good sense of self-worth. These women are go-getters and believe that being a Rose brings with it some extra kudos to who they are and I salute them.

The event has had a special place in the hearts of the Irish television public for many years with Brendan O'Reilly, Terry Wogan, Derek Davies, Ryan Tubridy, Ray D'Arcy and currently Dáithí Ó Sé presenting, not forgetting the leader of us all, Gay Byrne. My own presenter duties lasted six years and I can say, without fear of contradiction, that I absolutely loved them. It was such an amazing event, steeped in history, and it was truly a privilege to spend a week every summer in glorious Tralee. After the event in the dome I particularly loved the walk to the main street and the announcement from the back of the truck, sorry stage, that there was a new Rose. Splendid. For just one week in summer, we could be totally and utterly immersed in our Irishness and be proud of it.

...

The year after I took over as compère of the Rose of Tralee was to be memorable for sad reasons: the loss of my dad from cancer. He wasn't sick for long, only a few weeks, but his loss had a profound effect on me. We were the little family, Mam, Dad and me, and now he was gone. We nursed him at home and he died on 11 August 1998, after a particularly tough week. Knowing that he wouldn't make it, he told me he really wanted me to present the Rose. I decided that I wouldn't because I couldn't imagine doing the job under the circumstances, but he persisted and made me agree. I had no option. So it was that within a fortnight of my dad's passing, I found myself presenting the Rose of Tralee. My friend and colleague, Ian McGarry, said to me, 'You won't remember a minute of it, just go for it and let it happen, you'll be fine.' I suppose he was right. My actual memory of the night is clear in some ways, but most of it washed over me; what I do remember most clearly is the part Van Morrison played on that night.

To explain, I had loved his music for years, but during my dad's last few weeks, his songs took on a whole new meaning. I would stop and take stock, listen more attentively to his lyrics than I had ever done before and found my heart opening to his thoughts and his searching for meaning in this life and the next.

He has always been able to touch my heart with his words and beautiful music. I believe him to be a great poet who happens to write great music. I think back to *Moondance* and *Astral Weeks* and their impact but for Maria and me, albums like *A Sense of Wonder, Beautiful Vision, Poetic Champions Compose, Avalon Sunset* and *Inarticulate Speech of the Heart* rank among his finest. My particular choice of salve for my breaking heart around my Dad's passing was an album called *Enlightenment*. With lines like, 'Well I've been too long in this storm, I feel so sad and forlorn, and perhaps I'm counting on you. See me through.' Inspired. I played this album constantly during Dad's illness, his final days and after his passing. It had a huge impact on me and will always make feel close to my father.

Van provided the entertainment that night on the Rose of Tralee; he sang 'The Healing Game' and received a great reaction from the crowd in the dome on live television. The show went well and there was a bit of hospitality afterwards for the worker bees, a chance to relax and unwind and chat about the night's events, how it had gone, and have a glass or two to put the evening to rest. I was chatting to various people and it was all going splendidly and in walked Van Morrison with some people and sat down with me. I found him in chatty mood: we spoke about being only children, only sons and about the loss of our fathers, how our mothers coped and about the search for a higher power. We talked for the bones of an hour and I reflected on various of his songs that meant a lot to me and why. How the lyrics had spoken to me personally, how meanings that I had taken from songs sustained me in a time of pain and sorrow. He was attentive, expressive, interesting, witty, open; most surprising of all, not in any hurry to move off, but content to chat about things that interested us both. With the recent loss of my dad this encounter could not have occurred at a better time. I have to admit I was elated and emotionally drained by the end of it, but immensely grateful to Van for sharing his time.

Both Maria and I have met him over the years, in fact, most recently when he published a book of his lyrics, *Lit Up Inside*. I was invited by Van, along with the poet Michael Longley, to read two of his songs from the stage of the Olympia Theatre in Dublin. What a thrill. We've also attended his shows at the Culloden Hotel in Belfast, where he plays for two hours and the audience will be about 300 in total – intimate and stunning. I can't profess to know Van except in the sense that I'm a fan, I've read everything about him and I know his work intimately, but the Van I know, I like. I recommend that you let Van Morrison's music wash over you every now and then. You will be healed. He remains my greatest living troubadour and the artist who touches me like nobody else. He can touch your soul with his music if you let him.

Madama Butterfly
to Michael Bublé

If anyone had said to me that I would be broadcasting on radio on RTÉ Lyric FM I wouldn't have believed them, but then, in this business, you never know which way things can go. After *Open House* finished in 2004, I was invited by John Clarke, then head of 2fm, to come and chat, with a view to doing some work at the station. I duly returned to the breakfast show, working with Shane O'Donoghue, which was wonderful, but in a constantly evolving world, I wondered exactly how long it would last.

It was about a year and a half before the sands shifted. I had lunch with Adrian Moynes, director of radio at the time, and we talked of my plans. He knew I wanted to stay in RTÉ and yet I'd had a very substantial offer from outside, so what to do? He made the suggestion that I should consider Lyric FM. Initially, I thought he was joking, but he felt that I could make it my own. I wasn't sure that was possible but I was certainly sure that I liked the idea of it. And so, after some deliberation, I found myself presenting a Sunday afternoon show with a chap called Alan Ryan. We hit it off immediately and found a mutual joy in the Goons' humour, the Great American Songbook, his jazz pedigree and my singer-songwriter pedigree and our shared interest in the music of Ennio Morricone and Michael Bublé, as well as classical music. Just got on from the get-go. It was great fun for two hours on a Sunday afternoon. Of course, it required a boss to allow it to develop and this I found in Aodán Ó Dubhghaill. In any show like this you have to have people who trust your judgement and let you take risks that you know will pay off, and will give a show time to settle. Well, this he did, and there were some bumps along the way, but he believed in what we were trying to do, thank God.

We moved from Sunday afternoons to midday, Monday to Friday, and picked up a head of steam that led to *Marty in the Morning* from 7 to 10 a.m., Monday to Friday, with my wife ejecting me from bed some couple of hours earlier. This is the radio show that I've wanted to present all along.

Alan headed off to further his ambition with the BBC in the UK, so Sinead Wylde is now my producer, aided and abetted by Michael O'Kane, and the three of us bring it all to you for a very reasonable rate. It's so good to work with people you get on with, and we all 'get' each other. I miss

Alan's presence of a morning but I have Sinead and Michael and we are developing the show all the time, at least in me head!

I don't believe there is a breakfast show like it on radio anywhere; that's not a boast, it's just that we never really quite know where it will go. For the music, you could get everything from Puccini to Shostakovich to James Taylor to Elbow to Frank Sinatra to Willie Nelson to John Barry to Albinoni. Add to this the crazy letters I receive detailing anything from the perils of home decorating, to conversations about skinny-dipping in the west, the doings at Carlow College and the sleeping arrangements of the Gaye Jordans in Tuscany (apparently, their bed is divided in some Umbrian fashion ... I know), Neven Maguire joins us every Friday to put the hunger on us with his marvellous recipes, and of course, there are the jokes that help us make sense of the mornings. All of this topped off by the exploits of Hugo.

Now, for those of you who don't know him, Hugo inhabits a pile somewhere lush in Ireland with his wife (he's her second husband) Daphne, his mother-in-law Myrtle, various houseguests – Soledad from Barcelona, Randy from San Francisco – and various callers to their home. His first missive arrived out of the blue and I can honestly say that I have no clue as to his real identity. It's not me, I can assure you. I've never met him and I'd be afraid to, because he's absolutely a comic hero of mine. We get a blow-by-blow account of the family exploits and I only get to see it about 20 minutes before I read it live. It is truly a work of daftness and great humour and to my mind Hugo is a modern-day P. G. Wodehouse or Arthur Marshall. To those who don't remember him, Arthur Marshall was a comic genius, always with a touch of the *double entendre*. He might mention that he was out with his lobelias and his roses, and 'talk about pricks', he'd say, with a completely straight face. Hugo belongs to the same school of sly humour. The listener hangs on his every word and we never know from one day to the next what he's up to. But I love him and the joy he brings in the morning. That's why I like to read it live and discover his exploits along with the listener. If you'd like to get a flavour of the bould Hugo, well, look no further than the appendix to this book.

We also get to meet people along the way: Andrea Bocelli, opera singer Renée Fleming, Josh Groban, violinist Vladimir Jablokov, Rumer, composer David Arnold, Tony Bennett, Ennio Morricone, plus all the Irish greats like Celine Byrne, James Galway, Finbar Wright, etc. Then there are our opera trips to Verona with the listeners, and we've added Berlin and Prague to the list. Sinead works so hard to make these trips a reality and Michael is a great man for an itinerary. I am so spoiled by them. I always believed that such an undertaking would be popular with the *Marty in the Morning* gang and so it's proved. Plus, meeting the people I wake up in the morning is a boon and I can apologise in person over a drink in a Veronese bar!

There is also the moustache phenomenon. As one of the few … wait a minute, practically the only, moustachioed presenters around, I receive moustaches of all sorts: pens, glasses-holders, as well as false moustaches and ones that come in a different colour for every day of the week. I have a moustache for my bike, a moustache notebook, a door-stop, a throw for the couch and a full-sized mat for the hall. Dear heaven. Other entertainment comes in an off-the-cuff manner. I might have been somewhere the previous evening or seen some unusual photograph in the paper that triggers a response. In fact, during the summer-time, the very mention of me sporting a mankini generally causes a flood of texts and emails. They entreat me not to wear the dreaded garment, and yet, as it's luminous, I see that I would be in no danger, even in the evenings. There has even been a suggestion that I join the Dip in the Nip on the west coast in aid of cancer charities. Any time I seem to weaken and suggest that perhaps I *will* join them, there is an outpouring of offers to buy me gentleman's trunks. Perhaps they are right and I would only outshine others with my sporting physique! And so, I let it pass quietly. As my late father used to say: 'You, too, can have a body like mine if you're not careful.'

Breakfast time is about getting people in the mood to get up and out and set for the day, or, indeed, if the lie-in is called for, to make that pleasant, too. You can get your news if that's what you want – and I write as a newshound myself – but escapism is good for you...

Why, I had a communication only recently from C in Dublin:

Mart,

About ten years ago, I was working in Kildare and
we had a social outing one summer's evening. One
of the senior guys appeared in his casual gear, which
included a cap emblazoned with the words *National
Stud*. And I literally laughed into his face when I
saw it. Obviously, to the guys in Kildare, the words
have the horsey connotation but to a Dub like
myself, it would be quite unusual to see anyone with
a cap advertising the wearer as the *National Stud*.
The wearer was quite indignant at my giggles,
which only served to make it more hilarious.

Now, I was able to allay his fears and tell our intrepid correspondent in the wilds of Kildare that, in fact, I also possess
such a hat. I'm very careful where I wear it, don't want to
frighten the horses. And then I'm sliding into 'O Mio
Babbino Caro' from Puccini, and after, along comes listener
Regina Gargan with her funnies: 'Ticket inspectors, you
gotta hand it to them.' Or, 'I was walking in the park the
other day thinking, why does a Frisbee appear larger the
closer it gets, when it hit me.' I love it because it's the very
essence of people having fun first thing in the morning. One
joke begets another from someone else and so it goes on.

But, you cry, this is all very fine, this frivolity. But what of
the Greek question, for example, and serious matters such
as that? Well, as I dust down my trusty 45s from the mid-
seventies and prepare to share the warblings of Demis

Roussos, let us pause a while and ponder this, from Gerard Palmer of Dundrum:

> It is a slow day in a little Greek village. The rain is beating down and the streets are deserted. Times are tough, everybody is in debt and everybody lives on credit. On this particular day, a rich German tourist is driving through the village, stops at the local hotel and lays a €100 note on the desk, telling the hotel owner he wants to inspect the rooms upstairs in order to pick one in which to spend the night. The owner gives him some keys and as the visitor walks upstairs, the hotelier grabs the €100 note and runs next door to pay his debt to the butcher. The butcher takes the €100 note and runs down the street to repay his debt to the pig farmer. The pig farmer takes the €100 note and heads off to pay his bill at the supplier of feed and fuel. The guy at the farmers' co-op takes the €100 note and runs to pay his drinks bill at the taverna. The owner of the taverna had a night with his wife at the hotel so pops up to the premises and gives the €100 note to the hotel proprietor. The hotel proprietor then places the €100 note back on the counter so the rich traveller will not suspect anything.
>
> At that moment, the traveller comes down the stairs, picks up the €100 note, states that the rooms are not satisfactory, pockets the money and leaves town. No-one produced anything. No-one earned any-

thing. However, the whole village is now out of debt and looking to the future with a lot more optimism.

Now, that's what I call advice of a fiscal nature first thing in the morning. In fact, even if you look at that concept in the late afternoon, it seems to make sense. I think there might be a bit of a Greek in my correspondent, Mr Palmer!

...

I'm invariably asked how we put *Marty in the Morning* together. It might seem madcap and unplanned, with me out front and Sinead doing the producing, ably assisted by Michael, but there is a basic plan every day. Of course, it changes within minutes of going on air and that is as it should be, because we are reacting to the people who are listening. On sunny days, we might reach for the mankini and the factor 50, Italian tenors, 'Here comes the Sun' by the Beatles, or the great Lucio Dalla. When it rains, we acknowledge it and try to bring some sunshine moments to the morning. I find I can be taken down a completely different route by a story from a listener, happy or sad, that turns the programme, like an old ship, on a different course. But that's the pleasure of it all. The truth of it is, that at 7:10 on any given morning, we can all be enjoying the incredible music of Ludovico Einaudi or a little Verdi (say, 'Di Quella Pira', the tenor aria from *Il Trovatore*), or a trip down memory lane from Gilbert O'Sullivan, when a missive will arrive in and cause one of my detours on the wireless. Like the one recently about silence ... Are you sitting comfortably? Good, then I'll begin:

Once upon a time there was a prince who, through no fault of his own, was cast under a spell by an evil witch. The curse was that the prince could speak only one word each year. However, he could save up the words, so that if he did not speak one year, the following year he was allowed to speak two words.

One day, he met a beautiful princess and fell madly in love with her. With the greatest difficulty, he refrained from speaking for two whole years so that he could look at her and say 'my darling'. But at the end of these two years, he wished to tell her that he loved her. So he waited three more years without speaking, bringing the total number of silent years to five.

At the end of these five years, he realised that he had to ask her to marry him. So he waited another four years without speaking. Finally, as the ninth year of silence ended, his joy knew no bounds. Leading the lovely princess to the most secluded and romantic place in the beautiful royal garden, the Prince heaped a hundred red roses on her lap, knelt before her and, taking her hand in his, said, 'My darling, I love you. Will you marry me?' And the Princess tucked a strand of golden hair behind her dainty ear, opened her sapphire eyes in wonder and parting her ruby lips said … 'Pardon?'

Now follow that. Only 'The Sound of Silence' by Simon and Garfunkel seems apt.

Maria's dad was really the person who introduced us to classical music back in the day. My mam enjoyed light opera – Gilbert and Sullivan and the like. For years I thought *Naughty Marietta* was a bold biscuit! She loved Mario Lanza too, but Tom Dent loved opera. He played it at home, too, *Madama Butterfly* being his favourite. When both of them were slipping away from us years later we had opera playing in their hospital rooms; very sad, very poignant. When, through our shared love of opera, Maria and I discovered the joys of the Arena di Verona and those open-air operas on balmy Italian summer evenings, we often thought back to her dad and how much he would have loved it. It's such a joy to share that now with the Lyric listeners each year. We went for one of our big events (anniversary or birthday) and have returned almost every year since ... heavenly!

...

Of course, the people you work with are of vital importance in the overall blend of a radio show. Sinead, my producer, has a great knowledge of classical music but, like me, has dipped her toes in all sorts of musical waters. She is also a very organised person (thank God one of us is) and without her, the mornings could be a bit of a shambles. She has a great ability to corral. Michael, our broadcast assistant, brings his quirkiness to the table and I love quirkiness. We all get on so well. It's funny in this business how people are thrown together by a leader who obviously has an idea that they will get on and also that they bring different things to the table. Well, our leader Aodhán was correct here. Of course, we have to head out into the great radio unknown every morning and find people to share our mornings with. 'Simples' as a passing meerkat might say. 'Marty, I got eight legs of venison on Saturday for €30. Was that too dear?' Two deer! Heaven help us. And yet it shows that we have an ability to deal with consumer issues ... Yeah, right. Then there's a lady called Esther, who lives in Dublin 7, and any time I need something checked that I might have thrown out from the back of my brain, she is on it like a flash. She is our constant oracle on the northside of Dublin and I'd be a lesser man without her input.

I am the proud owner of a James Last cassette, thanks to Esther. Sadly, it won't play, but remains nonetheless in my office as a symbol of a great musical legacy left by the man from Bremen in Germany. That's the Lyric way, of course: we embrace music from all corners of the globe. Actually, with all the putdowns and the kitsch label that James Last suffered in this lifetime, it is worth noting that he sold more than 80 million albums, yet I don't know anybody who ever had one. Strange that. James Last knew his market and by virtue of playing to his perceived strengths, he succeeded. Not that he features a lot on the old request line, in contrast to a man who has taken on the mantle of leading an orchestra from the front: in this case, playing an instrument and dressed like a member of the Strauss family. I refer, of course, to the king of the castle, the knight of the Netherlands, our man in Maastricht ... André

Rieu. Or as the odd listener calls him, Andy Who. His success is actually phenomenal but he didn't lick it up, as the phrase goes; his dad was conductor of the Maastricht Symphony Orchestra, so it's in the genes.

...

Music has always been part and parcel of my life, and when Laura Allen from Universal Music came calling with an idea for a CD, I actually thought it was a joke. She got on to me a few times and then I met with her and the MD of Universal Music Ireland, Mark Crossingham. They basically asked me to put together a CD that represented my taste and the music I play on the show. How much of a thrill was that, do you think?

I was allowed to choose two sets of music, the first one the contemporary music we play, and the other one the classical/crossover material. I was like a child in a sweet shop and it took ages, with lists written and rewritten time and again. Then Universal Ireland had to go and try and find out could they get permission for various tracks; the whole process lasted months and months, but the people at the record company were brilliant and the list got the old whittle treatment and ended up as *Marty Recommends*, with a track listing of 34. Nearly all of my favourites are there, with two exceptions, Frank Sinatra and the Beatles, but even though some proved elusive, we still got Ella Fitzgerald, Elton John, Jimmy Webb, Van Morrison, Sammy Davis Jr and Glen Campbell, and on the other side Alfie Boe, Ennio Morricone, Ludovico Einaudi, Luciano Pavarotti, Julian

Lloyd Webber and Mícheál Ó Súilleabháin, among others. We've a song called 'Mama', the title of Chapter 2, if you'll remember, which I remember my mum buying for me back in 1966; there's 'Father and Son' from Cat Stevens. I recall on hearing that the first time how pleased I was that I had such a good relationship with my dad and that we had never fallen out. We've arias, the most famous cowboy theme of all and lots more.

I was overwhelmed by the goodwill that the CD attracted. This is all music I love, so to me, there is nothing unusual about the mix, but to some, it was an eye-opener (actually, an ear-opener). I am immensely proud of it and grateful to people like Chantal in Universal for promoting it so well. Did I mention it went to Number One in the Irish charts? Never realised I had so many relations.

...

Being able to get out of the studio from time to time is always a pleasure, because, quite frankly, otherwise I'd be left in the darkness, in the bowels of the earth at Radio Centre with cobwebs cascading down from my old yet trusty microphone. It's been a particular pleasure to find ourselves at the Bloom Festival in the Phoenix Park, at the National Ploughing Championships, at the Wexford Festival Opera and, never one to skip a breakfast (particularly from a Cavan man), our trips to my friend Neven Maguire at MacNean's of Blacklion. Being out and about requires a lot of preparation and Sinead and Michael are past masters at this – I tend to turn up in search of a decent room and an even more decent dinner, never a problem at Neven's. He is an exceptional man with extraordinary talent. Just looking at his menu makes me feel hungry … and a trip to Pat Henry's gym on the way home is always needed, and an extra notch on the belt for sure. We have broadcast from Neven's restaurant on a number of occasions and it's hugely popular, as is he. Mind you, he suggested at one time that I should cook on air at his own cookery school. I nipped that in the bud fairly lively. A friendly suggestion that he could present my show for an hour had my old pal scuttling back into the kitchen.

Our trips to the National Ploughing Championships have, to be honest, been boisterous. It's one of the biggest audiences in the country in terms of venues and we have great fun. We've even brought a band with us on a few occasions and that adds great atmosphere. Again, we are meeting the listener; after all, that's the point of the exercise. To be honest, I'm hardly likely to be in need of a combine harvester any time soon. But we knock great sport out of these occasions and as long as you have your wellies on standby, then all will be well.

At the championships, any number of people come up to me and talk about lineage; about meeting my dad in Clery's, my aunt who lived in Ferns, or the latest one I heard, about my brother in the midlands. This very attractive 25-year-old girl, a solicitor, told me about the marvellous evening she spent in his company. 'What a night we had,' she told me.

'Fascinating', I replied. 'I hope he was a gentleman in the course of the evening.' I was assured he was. That, at least, was a relief. The only thing is, I don't have a brother. I told her the truth, in as gentle a fashion as possible. Initially she seemed kind of shocked but then just brushed it aside and wondered did I have any Lyric FM hi-vis jackets. How easily these situations can be made good by the possibility of a hi-vis jacket.

Bloom is without question a glorious event, a sea of colour and a lovely event for Lyric FM particularly because we have the string quartet so people can relax on a nice Lyric FM seat and have goodies from our promotional department foisted upon them whether they want them or not. They nearly always do. It's a gorgeous day out where gardeners, garden suppliers, herbal maestros, purveyors of the finest lawn products and assorted businesses all come together for a feast of foliage, a cornucopia of chrysanthemums, an absolute diaspora of daffodils (oh, that's enough … Ed). The event lasts for five days and tens of thousands pour in to commune with nature.

Wexford Festival Opera offers us core Lyric FM values, but with a real twist. We broadcast from a shop in the town, down a lane from Wexford Opera House. The entrance to the opera house is just another doorway on a street of terraced houses, but once you enter it goes back and back and up and up. It's magical in its depth and a gorgeous building. A busy venue all year round, too. The event itself was founded by Tom Walsh in 1951 and has always put on works that hardly see the light of day from one end of the year to another, yet it works, and under David Agler as artistic director it continues to flourish. The ebullience of Elizabeth Rose-Browne as media relations manager adds such lustre to the occasion. She should be on the stage herself, she's such a character. She sent me a birthday greeting recently: 'A very happy birthday to you. I'm not saying you are old, but I'm just saying if you were milk … I'd smell you before I put you on my cereal'! How could you not warm to such a person? Love her ways.

The fact that we find ourselves in an empty shop or in the foyer of Whites Hotel being fed breakfast by Elizabeth when she's been up half the night says much for her dedication. Jeans one minute and tux the next, a typical day in Wexford town. Little would my grandfather, who was born in Clone, Ferns, Co. Wexford, and went on to work in Guinness at St James's Gate, have believed his grandson would be sitting with the great and the good at the opera. Not to mind in his native Wexford town. From this Martin Whelan to that Martin Whelan, I salute you.

…

If the show is anything it's an eclectic mix of the finest music we can find from all over the world, mixed with humour, good news stories and a lot of positivity. We live in a multi-choice world, and most of the news that comes our way is generally bad, so we try to counter that with an air of goodwill and offer up an oasis of calm in an otherwise boisterous world, both verbally and musically. Paddling our own canoe in an ocean that is less than calm, always and forever positive. Because there's always hope, as a story from a recent batch of post illustrates:

> Mart, here's a good one for you. There was a Scottish painter named Smokey McGregor, who was very interested in making a penny where he could, so he often thinned down his paint to make it go a wee bit further. He got away with this for some time, but eventually the local church decided to do a big restoration job on the outside of one of their biggest buildings. Smokey put in a bid and because his price was so low, he got the job. So he set about erecting scaffolding and setting up the planks, buying paint and yes, I am sorry to say, thinning it down with turpentine.
>
> Smokey was up on the scaffolding painting away, the job nearly completed, when suddenly there was a horrendous clap of thunder, the skies opened, and the rain poured down, washing the thinned paint from the church and knocking Smokey clear off the scaffold to land on the lawn among the gravestones. He was surrounded by tell-tale puddles of the thinned and useless paint.
>
> Smokey was no fool. He knew that this was a judgement from the Almighty, so he got down on his knees and cried, 'Oh, God, forgive me; what should I do?' And from the thunder a mighty voice spoke … 'Repaint! Repaint, my son, and thin no more!'

'That's Life'

Frank Sinatra

When in 1966, at the age of 10, I heard Cilla Black ask 'What's it All About, Alfie?' I had no idea of the answer. I suppose I would have assumed that, 50 years later, I might have some clue. Sadly, I'm not so sure I do. Of course, I've learned things over the years; I understand bits and pieces about lots of things; the passing years have seen joy and sorrow, loss and acquisition, pleasure and pain, and with all of this comes the realisation that much of what we do and who we are is transient. That is the way of the world and yet what *is* it all about?

I believe it's about striving to do the best you can, not always succeeding, and finding a way to try again and again and again until you do succeed. Because life isn't offered to us as a straight road, it's full of twists and turns and obstacles that need to be either removed or gotten around. What is it Elvis said about true love travelling on a gravel road? Life is handed to you, but the world doesn't owe you a living. When that particular penny drops it can be quite a revelation, but how you deal with it is the true test of your mettle and not always the easiest thing in the world to do.

The other realisation is that, quite often, the fact that your life has taken a different course, or become side-tracked, is not always your fault. This can make it easier to deal with: you didn't bring about the change, but, on the other hand, how on earth can you sort it out if you have no control over the issue in the first place? Now I'm beginning to drive myself mad.

So, even when things go cloudy and there's a bit of darkness around you, it's necessary to find the light in the midst of all that darkness. My philosophy, if I have one at all, is, as my friend Rory says, to always look on the bright side of life. That philosophy was taught to me when I was very small by my mum and dad and has been a rule of thumb all my life. Also, no matter what the world flings at you, self-belief is vital. Not easy when you're tested, and sometimes, to practise it, you'd need a neck like a jockey's, em, leather case.

Sometimes it's hard to believe that we actually possess the resilience we do, because it only surfaces when we are tested. We all hear stories about people in predicaments and we wonder how they were able to handle their situation and we think we couldn't do the same. Well, we can surprise ourselves. Obviously there are situations where some people just can't fight that fight and that's understandable because they are in a very dark place, and we must respect their vulnerability and try and protect them, but in the general run of things, there is always something we can do. I'm reminded of Frank Sinatra's great song, 'That's Life', about being down and out one month and on top of the world the next and how the great world keeps spinning nonetheless. Now, if you can find me a better song that gives you heart and a real sense of purpose, a feeling that I can do this, then I'd love to hear it because this one works fine for me. It's always been with me when times are tough and I've needed it for inspiration.

We all need things to hang on to when the road gets rocky: family, friends, faith – whatever gets you through the night. And so I start every day with the realisation that I'm alive, that each day brings new things and new things bring variety and variety is the spice of life! That might sound like a bit of nonsense but it works for me, so it's got some substance to it. Embrace the day, seize the moment, *carpe diem,* for those with the third-level ... This advice comes all the way from Horace's Odes, written in 23 BC, so really, very little has changed in a couple of millennia.

Life is also about pushing yourself, it's about self-motivation and realising that you've got to make the first move if things aren't going as you'd hoped and the plan isn't working. Time for a new plan! I'm reminded here of Mam and Dad's roses, which they cultivated by hand so lovingly; there were hundreds of them in the garden and Mam and Dad worked tirelessly on them to get them to produce so prodigiously; it took real care and attention and dedication to the task at hand. It's the same with anything: it's about effort; if you make the effort, quite often you reap the rewards. Now, life is not fair, as we know, so it doesn't always work out, but you've got to try.

Which reminds me, for some reason, of Mam's attempts to drive. She was very worldly wise and read voraciously, so she knew stuff about stuff. Yet for all her knowledge, she never learnt to drive. Well, that's *kind of* true. One day, my dad decided to give her a lesson down on Dollymount Strand in Clontarf where people have been driving for years, so it's not uncommon to see a learner out. My dad didn't bother with the L sign – why would you, he probably thought, she'd be driving in no time – I sat in the back, all set for the adventure, and away we went. Now, it was all a bit bumpy, jerky, if you like, but after a few dodgy starts, she got the hang of it. Then Dad, in his wisdom, suggested that she take a long drive along the beach to get used to steering. The only problem was that Dad had omitted two vital points of interest, if you are going to drive a car: first, the more you press down on the accelerator, the faster the car goes, and second – and to my mind the most important factor – the location of the brake. As my mother was unaware of either fact, she drove faster and faster in the general direction of the Irish Sea, with no concept of how to stop the car, roaring at my father, 'Where's the brake?' Only my father steering the car back inland and the handy placing of a clump of sand in the shape of a small sand dune made the car come to a shuddering halt. She never drove again. Happily they did, eventually, speak again. The point of this is, Mam had a go, in spite of her fears.

...

Life is also about faith. I've talked about my faith in God, but you also have to have faith in people around you. Life happens and things happen that you can't control, but having people around you whom you believe in and can depend on is very important. My first producer in television was Niall Matthews on *Thirty Years a Poppin'* all those years ago and my best man and longest-standing friend in broadcasting, Robbie Irwin, set the questions for the quiz. We are all still good. In fact, Niall's last production position in RTÉ was on *Winning Streak,* and it's been good to have people around me who make the job more special. Company it's good to keep. My agent is a wonderful woman called Carol Hanna, whom I've known since she worked in the office of Tommy Hayden when we all started out on 2fm. We have known each other all that time and I trust her implicitly. As the years passed, we've become friends and remain so. I would never knowingly let her down, nor she me, and there is a comfort in that. I know that she will only book me out to events that are appropriate and I know she's in my corner. We've both had events in life where our friendship was called upon and it's accurate to say that it's really when trouble comes that your true friends step up to the mark for you.

It's true that when I went through my various job changes, people came and went along the way. It's also true that when I was off the wireless, the phone stopped ringing, and it was at this time that I realised the value of my friends. I had thought that some people were friends, and the realisation that they weren't, and had moved on, was quite hard to take. If you've lost your job and are clearly out on a limb, then your hope would be that people you have looked out for over the years will be there for you when things get tough. Well, you make that assumption at your peril. Maybe I was innocent or just naïve, but at the time it hurt and even recalling it now, I remember it as a horrible time. Still, I was fortunate that enough people were there for me and we overcame the obstacles.

Bill Hughes has been my friend since 1985. A brighter, more fun man it would be impossible to find; a bear of a man. Along with our good and pure friendship, he and I have also worked together on occasions, including two seasons of *Celebrity Jigs and Reels*, where well-known people were taught Irish dancing and then appeared on TV in competition, not always with great results. It was great television and we had more than our fair share of a great time together. We love his friendship and we've shared many nights at dinner tables over the years and laughed the night away. So too, with Gary Kavanagh, also a friend of ours for 30 years. He has been a director of Peter Mark and his talent is legendary. His sense of *joie de vivre* and friendship has also added so much to our lives. In our conversations, no one is safe and the libel courts would be full if anybody heard our chats over the years. Warmth, caring, fun, actually a wicked sense of humour ... Gary has all of these qualities, and he's the man who kept me dark until I saw the light and went *au naturel.**

I can't write this book without mentioning *Celebrity Bainisteoir*, and having taken part in that great TV experience, it's hard to believe I had the chance to coach a GAA team from the midlands, Maryland from Co. Westmeath, and went on to win the series. The fact that I won it against one of my biggest friends, Gerald Keane, gave me particular pleasure and I never cease to remind him of it. 'And by the way, here I go again.' He'll know what this means.

...

On the topic of friendships, I recall a trip we made with Pauline and Pat, our best friends from back in the day, which could only have been undertaken with true friends.

---

* At least now there are flowing locks thanks to Maurice Collins and his fine team at HRBR, while the top make-up girl in RTÉ Margaret Curran used her considerable talent to ensure that having had the op on a Monday, I was on *Winning Streak* on that Saturday and nobody noticed – what a genius. Having a hair transplant made me feel better almost immediately and I have no regrets about it, only a sense of having done the right thing and being happy with it every day. It grows on you, you know.

Maria had known them both from Aer Lingus, so they were seasoned travellers, and we all determined to go on an adventure together. So, it's 1987 and let's see, where shall we go, we thought. Why not somewhere that's currently got a dodgy reputation and should be really interesting, if not slightly dangerous. Let's go to Peru! Where the Shining Path (Sendero Luminoso) were in full flow and causing all sorts of bother by fighting a guerrilla war against the government.

Peru it was and our first stop was the capital, Lima. We were staying in a nice hotel, and all was well, until the concierge told us, 'It's all fine around here, but if you're going out, turn left, not right. When you leave here, don't even contemplate turning right.' Quite what awaited us if we turned right, we didn't know, but Lima was beautiful and all went well. We had a few peculiar incidents, one of which occurred on the highway when we were driving our hired car from Lima to Miraflores. We were pulled in at a checkpoint and the four of us had to go into the office. There, policemen, and I use the term loosely, dressed in open-necked shirts and jeans and packing guns, went through our papers, passports et cetera. They spoke Spanish the entire time, all the while looking at Maria and Pauline and making comments which I'm sure were as pure as the driven snow. Very, very intimidating, especially when none of us spoke Spanish: one of us had German, two of us had French and the other one had an inordinate need to pee. It took an age and they eventually let us go, but it was quite scary.

We took the tourist train to Cusco, with armed tourist police on board, but it was a beautiful journey and made all the more special by the locals with their wonderful colourful outfits and chatty ways – among themselves; we couldn't understand a word. Now, Cusco is situated in the southern Andes and was once capital of the Incan Empire. The thing you need to understand is that it is one of the highest places you are likely to visit ... so what's the first thing you do when you've booked into your hotel with your pals? That's right, having no thought at all to the fact that you are now 3399 metres (11,152 feet in old money) above sea level, you light cigarettes. To say that nausea came over us in the space of 30 seconds is not to exaggerate. The smoke came out so fast, I thought I was going to take off. Sick as a parrot fairly lively and then a bit of a lie-down.

Actually, Maria was badly affected by the altitude sickness, but the important thing is we made it to Machu Picchu, the 15th-century Inca site and the largest tourist attraction in South America. Machu Picchu was built at the height of the Inca Empire in 1450 and abandoned a hundred years later, but it wasn't discovered again until a historian by the name of Hiram Bingham III met a couple who were farming some of the agricultural terraces when he was on an expedition in the area in the early 20th century, and the rest is history. It really is a must-see and was recently voted one of the new Seven Wonders of the World.

We even had time to visit Iquitos, commonly known as the capital city of the Amazon, for a couple of days, where Pat and I decided to swim with piranhas in the Amazon River. Our guide, Anselmo, assured us that they wouldn't attack us unless there was blood in the water: that was the shortest swim ever.

We had a lovely relaxing week, then, at the end of our holiday in an enclosed compound in the posh part of town, where the porters carried guns and there was a perimeter fence around the length of the whole complex. Lovely! But the fun didn't stop there. We went home earlier than Pauline and Pat, who remained in Lima for a few extra days. I had to get back to the radio, so we had a standby flight out of Lima one evening to Miami and then on. There was a curfew from 9 p.m., so nobody went out on the streets, which were patrolled by the army in armoured personnel carriers. The flight was full and we weren't getting on and there was one jumpseat available, which, it was being suggested, I take, as I had work commitments. What, I thought, and leave Mrs Whelan on her own in the airport with a curfew outside? No way. So at check-in, I mustered whatever remaining Peruvian currency I possessed (along with dollars) which seemed to slip into my passport as I suggested to the clerk at the counter that they might like to check again just in case there was another seat. Mercifully there was and we ran for the plane and made it by the skin of our teeth. There, I sat on one of the crew seats and Maria took her place in the cockpit. Now, that was some adventure.

I remember others as well on this trip: the internal flight in Peru where they played bingo on board and we thought this was hilarious (pre-Ryanair); as we got onto the plane, the air hostess, with very little English, said the same thing to everybody boarding; 'Back door, nice trip'. It's become a catchphrase with all of us.

The trip with our friends brought us closer together and that continues with Jessica and Thomas being firm friends with Pauline and Pat's boys, Jack and Matthew. We also have the most amazing long-distance relationship with our friends in Boston, Wayne and Loie. Maria first met Wayne in 1975, when she went to visit her Aunty Eileen in Boston, and they've been friends ever since. Maria's aunt was our Irish connection in America and we have stayed with her many times and enjoyed her hospitality and friendship. That's where our love affair with America started: in Massachusetts all those years ago.

Wayne and Loie are the warmest, most giving people and we love their company. We go to them and they come to us, bringing with them the finest sour cream known to man and a product for coffee called half-and-half: we reciprocate in a similar vein. We've had some lovely times with them in Boston, but also on Nantucket Island, a gorgeous spot 30 miles south of Cape Cod. In fact, when the children were younger, Wayne and Loie used to mind them along with their son, Christopher, while Maria and I headed off to the island that we absolutely adore, Martha's Vineyard. Once you arrive at Vineyard Haven and head off into the body of the island, you know for sure you're completely and utterly away from the world as we know it. I love the sparseness of Menemsha and the sunsets only God could create, so beautiful. We went out on a boat once in Martha's Vineyard, which was skippered by James Taylor's brother. It's what he does, but it seemed so surreal. I wanted to break into 'Fire and Rain' or 'Sweet Baby James', but held my fire until we were out of earshot. Then I went for it.

On a couple of occasions we have shared a house with Wayne and Loie and their friends Missy and Bill from New Jersey and their girls, and another friend, Jan-Jan from New York, so that's a total of 12 of us. But this is no ordinary house; it's a beautiful olde worlde wooden construction built on Squam Lake in New Hampshire. An idyllic location to really and truly turn off, it's also known as the home of the loon, so I felt right at home! (It's a type of bird, just so you know. They make an incredibly haunting, plaintive noise and when they mate, they do so for life ... bit like myself.) Squam Lake is best known as the location for the film *On Golden Pond* with Henry Fonda, Jane Fonda and Katherine Hepburn, a wonderful film which will do your heart good.

On a holiday like this we are thrown together so we all muck in and great dinners are prepared and washed down with a glass or two of Zinfandel or a cheeky white. A glass or two of Old Grand-Dad also finds its way to the table. These holidays are so special: watching the children learn to water-ski, sitting around and talking into the late evening, enjoying a table tennis tournament, kayaking (needless to remark, I fell in) and even our very own disco night. There's no air-conditioning and the bugs like to say hello of an evening, but it doesn't spoil the atmosphere of a location so blessed that you just feel that it's great to be alive when you are there. There's also the matter of an outdoor shower ... happily, there's not a camera in sight. We all row in financially and workwise and it's a special place, with special friendships forged over so many years.

...

I do a lot of charity work and enjoy giving back in thanks for the good things that have come my way in life. I've such admiration for committees and individuals who dedicate so much time and effort to organising events, big and small. For those involved, all events are major and there are good people everywhere. Some like my friend Miriam Hand (Breast Cancer Research Ireland) are super at their jobs, and so dedicated. I also support the Irish Heart Foundation, Stroke Support, the marvellous work of Des and Dr Susie O'Connell with orphans in Moldova, the Carers' Association and many more. I do what I can and thank God for my good health and that of my family.

But there are those who find themselves fundraising through tragedy visiting their lives. One such family are our friends Don and Sandra Nugent. Don and I met many years ago when he was working in Switzers department store on Grafton Street and I was doing an outside broadcast for 2fm from the shop window (technically that's an inside broadcast!). We hit it off immediately and became firm friends. They're two amazing people, very similar to

Maria and I. Happily married for 30 years, with two beautiful children, Emma and Ross, older sister, younger brother; just like us, a content and happy family.

Tragedy struck their family, however, when their gorgeous, talented and bright boy Ross took ill. Initially he had dreadful back pain and weight loss; he was subsequently diagnosed with a rare cancer called Ewing's Sarcoma. How do you cope as parents or siblings with that devastating news? Ross fought his illness with such bravery and stoicism. He was so insightful about life and what was going on around him. During his illness and treatment at Beaumont hospital, he noticed that the blood pressure monitors the nurses were using sometimes couldn't get an accurate reading for him and they would have to keep trying. He said one day to his mam and dad that 'when' (not 'if') he got better, he would fundraise to get some 'high-tech monitors' for the oncology ward. The seed was sown for the Ross Nugent Foundation (RNF). The mission of the Ross Nugent Foundation is to provide equipment to make life more comfortable for cancer patients, visiting relations and nursing staff in Beaumont and other hospitals.

Sadly and tragically Ross left this world on 15 May 2010, leaving behind a mam, dad and sister with such a void in their world and pain in their hearts. Their loss will be there always and they will carry him in their hearts forever. But Don, Sandra and Emma have put their sorrow to great use and have over the last five years worked so hard to raise funds for the oncology ward at Beaumont, St Clare's, where Ross was cared for. They got the monitors, and electric beds, and ergonomic stools, and physiotherapy, and now a fully equipped chill-out room for patients and visitors alike. On each piece of equipment is a logo (which Ross created) and his presence can be felt every day.

Every penny goes towards buying equipment for the ward and the family are guided by the nurses and doctors and their requirements. Ross would have been so proud of his wonderful parents and friends who have helped fulfil his promise. I help in any way I can. I knew Ross and liked him very much. He was a special boy and at 18, on the verge of manhood, taken too, too soon. Whatever the foundation asks me to do, I do. He deserves nothing less.

...

We are very lucky, Maria and I, to have friends near and far, people to share time with. We have friends who have lost loved ones along the way, just like us. We have friends who don't have the trappings they used to have, we have friends who have broken up, we have friends who didn't seem affected by the recession and we have friends who were totally affected by the recession. The important thing is, we have friends. There are those I'd like to see more of and I'm always determined that I will, but life comes along and other things get in the way – there is always something. Finding the time, that's the trick, and it's worth it.

On the subject of friends, it might seem a bit strange to count a dog as a friend, but such is the case with a big ball of black and white wool called Buddy, a border collie who has lived with us all his life (Buddy Collie ... geddit?). He is the most lovable, kind and caring dog you can imagine. Now, his job is to herd livestock, particularly sheep, but since we don't have any, he has herded us around all his life. He is obedient, he is clever and he loves us with a passion. When he gets us all into one room he tends to curl up at the door, his job done. He has never been any trouble to us except obviously when he was a pup and destroyed our home for weeks on end. Then one day he suddenly calmed down and sweetness and light prevailed.

I never had a dog when I was small, even though somewhere in the dark recesses of my mind, I believe I did! My current wife believes it has something to do with reading Enid Blyton books, particularly the *Famous Five*, where there was a dog named Timmy, the same as my imaginary dog.

Buddy came to us from Donegal and had a lovely soft Gweedore accent ... I'm joking! But what he did have, and what he stole immediately, were the hearts of my children, then Maria's and, eventually, mine – I was never a doggy person and it took me quite a while to adapt to his presence, but when I did, I was a goner.

We get cards and letters from people who address their correspondence to the four of us and Buddy, that's how much a part of our family he is. For many years, when we lived in Portmarnock, Maria walked the beach known the Silver Strand, with Buddy, and he would run and run as if he didn't know how to stop (sounds like the mother in the car learning to drive). He loved those runs and would always act in such an excited fashion before heading off for his walk.

Apparently, all pure border collies trace their ancestral line back to a dog called Old Hemp, born in 1893 in Northumbria and a natural with the sheep. Well, Buddy is a natural with us and we love him, but ailments he's carried for some time are beginning to affect him and old age is simply taking its toll. Some border collies live to be 17, that's 119 in our years, but our Buddy is 15 and that's 105, so let's deal with that while we can. His has been a charmed life, where his function has been to love and be loved. We will mind him for as long as he is able to stay, but there's life in the old dog yet.

...

We had dreamed of building our own house for years and years to the point where we had so many books on building styles and options the old house was beginning to sag to one side with the weight. Initially we bought our site – we were one of the first to buy, and then practically the last to build. Why? The vagaries of this business. In fact it seemed there was never going to be a right time for us, so eventually we just went for it. Mad or what? A friend pushed us forward and I'm so glad he did. When we did build we discovered our neighbours on either side shared our names; on one side were the Martins and on the other were the Whelans, and there we were bang smack in the middle of the two of them. On top of that we had always wanted to call our home Avalon. No chance – the Whelans got there before us. Pity the postman, so we await a name.

But I'm so glad we built our house. Maria dreamt it up and we went for it. Over a long period, Liam Tuite and Fran Whelan added their expertise and style and one day, all of a sudden, there it was and we love it. It's home, it's where the heart and hearth is. Home. Where love lives and the ones who truly care embrace every day and each other.

If it hadn't been for that push we would never have proceeded. It took a friend with knowledge and confidence to give us the all-important nudge to move forward. Sometimes that's all you need from a pal.

...

So, friends are essential in life, but as I reach a certain stage, I begin to look back as much as forward and I realise that so many people have gone. My parents, Maria's parents; on my mother's side, all her siblings are gone; Mam's sister Evelyn passed in London a few years ago. On Dad's side, only one sister remains, my Auntie Rita, Kay having passed away a few years ago. Auntie Rita and Auntie Kay were fab and doted on me (and why wouldn't they?). I recall my two aunts taking me to see Santa at Christmas time and I also remember Auntie Rita and her late husband Tom calling to my parents' house on Hallowe'en, before they had their own children. They were dressed up in full Hallowe'en costumes and refused to take their masks off. Even though my parents were not quite sure that it was Tom and Rita, they let them in. They also lived a normal life, producing two lovely children, Anne and Paul, just in case you're wondering. Between all my parents' siblings there are only seven children; I make eight cousins all in. We couldn't even make up a team for mixed soccer. A tiny grouping, so the losses are really noticed.

Inevitably, if you hang about long enough, you will lose family, friends and colleagues along the way. My life is no different. I carry the losses with me as lightly as possible but the loss of people I care about cuts deep. So friendship matters all the more.

Maria and I are blessed to have good friends, people we can rely on and who can rely on us. It's interesting but I have never been a clubby person, so when I play tennis, I play the game and then I head off – I don't hang around the clubhouse. I've never had the time to give to golf that you need to if you are to be any use and so I don't pull in friendships from those quarters like others do. But that's fine, too, because the only child will always be content in his own company. Not lonely, just comfortable. I have a major failing, though, and it's the phone. I rarely answer it, which is not very clever considering how useful a tool it is in my career and I'm awful at getting back to people. I'm trying to get better, but unfortunately I'm notorious. When I'm focusing on a particular job at hand or looking at a new project or preparing tomorrow's programme or whatever and the phone rings, it gets in the way. So it goes to voicemail and I vow to get back to whoever called. By the end of the day there could be 17 missed calls and a dozen messages. In an age of instant communication and decisions made on the hop, this is hardly clever. I really need to sort it out. And while we're on the topic of telephones, here's one of my favourite jokes. Cecily phoned Directory Enquiries and asked for the number of a knitwear company in Woven. The operator asked, 'Woven? Are you sure? There's no knitwear company there that I can find.'

'Yes,' Cecily responded, 'that's what it says on the label of my jersey – Woven in Scotland.'*

...

I start very early in the morning for the radio show and generally I'm in by about a quarter to six. I like to set out my stall for the three hours ahead from seven until 10. Equipped with my CDs, papers, post from the lovely listener and my trusty Beano flask of piping hot coffee, I'm ready for the off with Sinead and Michael as we sally forth into the day. However, one morning not so long ago, I found myself standing in the radio centre and a strange sensation came over me. I suddenly realised that the first time I had stood here was in 1979. That was 36 years ago, and I have no idea where all those years went. You can imagine at that time of the morning there wasn't a sound in the

---

* I know, the silly ones are sometimes the best ones. Which also reminds me of the gag Fiona in Celbridge cheered me up with the other morning on the wireless; Q: What do you get when you cross a sheep with a kangaroo? A: A woolly jumper.

place and the silence only added to the moment. I was so taken aback by the sensation I had to sit down and take it all in. I looked around me and saw the ghosts of presenters past, bosses who loved me and bosses who couldn't or wouldn't relate to me. I remembered some of the music we played, all on vinyl. I remember bringing down a box of cartridges on which were the RTE Radio 2 jingles, and my friend and producer Robbie with his smiling face.

For a few moments I was back at the tail end of 1979, as Van Morrison would say: back, way, way back. Back before the Eurovision Song Contest, back before the Rose of Tralee, back before Lyric FM, back before *Open House*, *Fame and Fortune*, *Winning Streak*. Back before my beautiful children Jessica and Thomas … back, back, back. And all the while, I was striving to be successful, to do the best I could and to make it all work somehow. I do the best with my career so that the people I love can have as good a life as possible, but I also do the best with my career for myself, like many people. Because pride in what you do is very important; it doesn't matter what it is, as long as you have pride in it. So every day, I give it my best shot and hope that I entertain some people along the way, that's all I can do. I hope as I've gone through (and I'm not finished by a long shot) that I have been able to bring some merriment into the lives of people and lift them out of what might otherwise have been a gloomy day.

As time has eased by and the passing years teach their lessons, I know for sure that all of us are shortly forgotten. Even people who are well known don't stay that long in the public consciousness when they're gone. The exceptions are people who create; painters, musicians, singers, poets, sculptors, writers and the rest of the artistic fraternity, who leave work to live on after them. I still read and reread the humour of Alan Coren and Spike Milligan, the political brilliance of Theodore H. White on American politics; I play and listen to the music of Frank Sinatra, Van Morrison, Ella Fitzgerald, John Martyn; I read the poetry of W. B. Yeats, etc. They leave a legacy that is their craft, their art, their brilliance. For the rest of us, if we are lucky, we'll be remembered for about a fortnight.

But to those we loved and those who loved us, well, my expectations stretch to something a bit longer. Because really it's the love shared that matters. It's the people with whom I share love who will take me with them for some time yet. I know that I was lucky to have two of the most beautiful children imaginable and, because of the first real bit of perseverance in my life, I was able to get the girl of my dreams and to hold her fast for all these years. Maria. Every day it's like I've just met a girl called Maria. What is it Lennon and McCartney say about the love you take and the love you make? In the end they are equal. Now, *that's* life.

APPENDIX

Hugo's Letter to *Marty in the Morning*

...

Music: Katherine Jenkins singing 'Parla Più Piano'
(the love theme from *The Godfather* by Nino Rota)
on her album *Believe*.

My dear Marty,

It was a typical Sunday evening after the dinner, with the lot of us in the Blue Drawing Room, the 50-inch TV switched on, and the sound turned down. This, I find, is the best way to watch telly; it doesn't interrupt conversation quite so badly. I'm sure it's much the same in Whelan Mansions.

Now, it's not often that we have both my musical sister Imogen and Daphne's ne'er-do-well brother Ashley in the house at the same time. Indeed, some uncharitable people have wondered aloud if one might be the other in drag, but there's none of that in our family. My sister Imogen is, as you may know, Marty, the third best cor anglais player in Ireland. Of Daphne's brother, Ashley, well, the less said the better, I find.

'Is there any sign of that young Soledad one?' said Ashley. *'I'm gasping for a cup of tea.'*

'She's upstairs helping Tadeusz with his Dangling Participles,' said Daphne.

'Isn't she very good!' said Heather.

'Is he having trouble with them?' said Ashley.

'He is, all right.'

'*Do you know, I thought that, listening to him,*' said Ashley.

'*It's sticking out a mile.*'

'*Has she training in that area?*' I asked.

'*She's feeling her way with his syntax,*' said Daphne. '*It's a matter of some wonder what she can achieve with that young Pole, but he seems to be thriving on it, linguistically.*'

'*Oh, he is, Daphne,*' Myrtle said, refilling her sherry glass. '*Whatever she's doing with him is really adding to his fluency.*'

'*He has a great grasp of the tongue, all right, for a non-native speaker,*' Heather said. '*Soledad can be proud of that.*'

'*I wish I had my instrument to hand now, to test my own tongue technique,*' Imogen murmured, as if to change the track of the conversation subtly in her own direction. '*I long to hear the plaintive note of the cor anglais.*'

'*Are you giving any public recitals these days, Imogen?*' asked Mick the Chemist.

'*No, Michael,*' she replied. '*I'm on stand-by in case of any emergency Dvořák in the NCH over the winter, but otherwise I'm resting. Would you go if I was playing?'*

'No, I'm waiting for the next piano recital by that Alfred Brendel from the Continent,' Mick said. *'I don't like to overdo the heavy stuff.'*

'Quite right too, Mick,' said Daphne. *'At your age it doesn't do to over-exert yourself. What's that on the television there, Hugo?'*

'Some trashy soap opera, love. All butlers and nobs and valets and under-housemaids.'

'Did you never think of employing a valet yourself, Hugo?' asked Myrtle.

'Oh, no. I like to live simply,' I said. *'I've no airs and graces.'*

'That's true,' said Myrtle, rattling out her copy of the *Sunday Independent*. *'None. No airs and certainly no graces. And it's years since I've had as much as a truffle sandwich in this house.'*

'It's the simple life, Myrtle,' I said.

'Do you know, Daphne, I can't believe what this one here in the paper has been up to,' Myrtle said, ignoring me.

'*Keep it to yourself, Mummy,*' Daphne said. '*I like to take the* Sindo *to bed.*'

'*What would I do with a valet anyway?*' I asked.

'*I could show you, Mr Hugo, sir,*' said Randy. '*Living in high style in Italy. We could go on the Grand Tour together.*'

'*You'd get truffle sandwiches then,*' Myrtle said. '*And prosecco. And Parma ham. And tiramisu. And gelato. And limoncello.*'

'*I suppose your own wedding, Randy, if it ever comes, will be like George Clooney's wedding in Venice,*' I said.

'*Venice?*' said Mick. '*Do you know they call Venice "the Cork of the South"?*'

'*Of the East!*' his wife Heather corrected him. '*Florence is the Cork of the South.*'

'*Ah!*'

'*Has George Clooney taken a woman into his life?*' Randy asked, picking up the threads of a fragmented conversation.

'Yes, *Randy, late in life. There's hope for everyone in that, you know,*' Ashley said. '*Did you hear that, Imogen? George Clooney has married at a great age.*'

'*Does he play an instrument?*' Imogen asked, with her relentlessly one-track mind.

'*I'm sure he does, Imogen,*' Ashley replied, '*but probably only in the privacy of his own lounge. Perhaps the flute, like Sir James and Lady Galway.*'

'*I've love to be sitting on the couch with a man like Gorgeous George,*' said Heather.

'*That can't be true about Katherine Jenkins!*' Imogen exclaimed, looking up from the headline in the *Mail on Sunday.*

'*Is what true?*'

'*You know: that she's got married!*'

'*It's in the paper today,*' said Myrtle. '*I read it earlier when I was upstairs.*'

'*How extraordinary!*' said Imogen.

'*Did someone say George Clooney is getting married?*' Jolyon asked, laying the Style section of the

Farmers' Journal aside on an occasional table that we believe once belonged to Maria Edgeworth, the novelist. *'I thought someone said George Clooney got married.'*

Myrtle dropped the sherry glass she had been toying with whilst reading the Sunday rags.

'George Clooney has got married?' she said.

'Yes,' said Daphne.

'How appalling!' said Soledad, who just then entered the Blue Drawing Room, with Tadeusz in tow.

'To a woman?' said Myrtle.

'Well, yes, of course to a woman, Mummy. Obviously.'

'I could go grey with the shock,' said Myrtle.

'Why, Mummy?'

'Well, I'd always thought if we were to meet that he might be swept off his feet by the sight of me.'

'I could imagine that, Myrtle,' I said.

'Don't be so silly, Mummy!' said Daphne.

'Well, Daphne, I haven't given up on the prospect of remarriage, you know. For the right man.'

'He's found love, Myrtle,' Mick said.

'I had an eye on him,' she replied. 'In case I'd marry again. He was a definite possibility. Distinguished.'

'And rich!' said Heather.

'Is he?' said Myrtle.

'Was it his wolfish good looks, Mummy, that tempted you?' Ashley asked.

'Oh, no.'

'Or his salt-and-pepper hair?' said Heather.

'Oh, no, not at all.'

'What was it then?' Daphne asked.

'His money, Daphne. I felt I could do justice to it. Easier than a big win on Winning Streak. This is most disappointing.'

She shifted uneasily on her Edwardian lady's chair, and made to get up.

'Are you off, Myrtle?' I asked.

'*I'm going upstairs to take off my hat, Hugo,*' she said. '*I am not at all pleased,*' and she waddled out of the Blue Drawing Room.

'*Daphne,*' I said, '*your mother isn't wearing a hat.*'

'*And?*' said Daphne.

'*Ah!*' I said.

There was a lull in the conversation and the telly got turned up a bit for a while.

'*Is there any chance you might surprise us your-self, Jolyon?* said Ashley. '*When you doff those lavender shirts.*'

'*In what way, Uncle Ashley?*' said Jolyon.

'*By marrying an heiress.*'

'*No, Uncle Ashley, most unlikely,*' said Jolyon.

'*Our Jolyon is a real Lothario, aren't you Jolyon?*' said Daphne. '*Drives the girls wild!*'

'*Hmmm,*' said Myrtle, returning to the Drawing Room, hatless, and looking no happier than she had left it.

'*Are you all right there, Mother?*' said Heather.

'*I blame him,*' Myrtle said, pointing at me. '*He's trying to do me in!*'

'*Who, Mother?*' said Daphne.

'*That husband of yours. I nearly came to grief upstairs.*'

'*What happened, Mummy?*' said Heather.

'*You'd need to get that seat fixed up there, Daphne. There's a screw loose.*'

'*That doesn't surprise me,*' I said quietly.

'*I didn't know that, Mummy,*' said Daphne. '*About the screw.*'

'*Yes, Daphne. I nearly took off out the door and down the stairs as soon as I sat down. I could have landed here downstairs amongst the lot of you watching the telly.*'

'*How appalling!*' said Soledad.

Yours truly,
Hugo

LIST OF CHAPTER PHOTOS

'Dancing in the Dark'
Dancing with Bruce Springsteen on the 4th of July.

'Mama'
With Mam and Dad in Stratford-upon-Avon.

'Band on the Run'
The happy drummer with Leo Conway, Kevin Murphy, Brendan Lyons, Declan Brannigan and the late Óisin Healy.

'When Will I See You Again'
Engaged … young love.

'Something in the Air'
2fm; Larry, Jimmy, Gerry, Jim and Philip (© *RTÉ Stills Library*).

'Cycles'
With Terry Wogan at radio business.

'Wichita Lineman'
With Mary Kennedy on *Open House*.

'Heroes'
With Maria and David Bowie at Slane.

'The Special Years'
Our young family.

'What's Another Year'/'Hold Me Now'
The opulence of a Eurovision commentator's booth.

Madama Butterfly to Michael Bublé
With Lyric FM's Sinead Wylde and Michael O'Kane in my beloved Arena di Verona.

'That's Life'
Maria, Jessica, Thomas and I waiting for the train in Malahide!